James McNair's Cakes

Recipes by James McNair
and Andrew Moore

Photographs and Styling
by James McNair

CHRONICLE BOOKS
SAN FRANCISCO

Library of Congress Cataloging-in-Publication Data:
McNair, James K.
    [Cakes]
    James McNair's Cakes/photographs and styling
    by James McNair.
        p.   cm.
    Includes index.
    ISBN 0-8118-1768-7 (pbk.)
    1. Cake. I. Title. II. Title: Cakes
TX771.M318   1999
641.8'653—dc21
                                        98-31677
                                        CIP

Printed in Hong Kong.

Editorial and photographic production by James McNair and Andrew Moore, The Rockpile Press, San Francisco and Lake Tahoe, California

Designed by Brenda Rae Eno

Distributed in Canada by Raincoast Books
8680 Cambie Street
Vancouver, British Columbia V6P 6M9

10 9 8 7 6 5 4 3 2 1

Chronicle Books
85 Second Street
San Francisco, California 94105
www.chroniclebooks.com

For my "niece" Malia Pearl Forbert, who calls me Happy Cakes and always expects me to have a cake in hand. And for her parents, Maile and Mark Forbert, who are generous, supportive, and caring members of my extended family.

And in memory of three uncles who departed while I was working on this book:

Uncle Victor Holstead of Winnsboro, Louisiana, was a gentle, soft-spoken man who always listened to me as a child and showed genuine interest in my adult life and career.

Uncle Sanford Keith of Jackson, Mississippi, was blinded in an accident shortly before I was born. Despite that misfortune, he ran a successful food-service business where I sometimes served as a helper in my youth. I always admired his ability to maintain a sense of humor in spite of a handicap that would have defeated many people.

"Uncle" Bill Gallagher of Pleasant Hill, California, welcomed me into his extended family from the first day I met him and remained one of my greatest supporters. For his memorial gathering, I baked the Heirloom Apple Cake on page 75 from delicious apples grown in his backyard.

Props on the listed pages have been graciously loaned by the following merchants.
Dandelion, San Francisco: 38, 80, 82, 95, 96, and 99.
Fillamento, San Francisco: cover, 22, 29, 49, 50, 53, 62, and 66.
KNF Designs and Vietri from Frank Maxwell & Associates, San Francisco, available from Vanderbilt & Company, St. Helena, California, and other fine stores: 69, 71, and 79.

Contents

Happy Cakes

My young "niece" Malia Pearl Forbert calls me Happy Cakes, a title that I accept with great pride. The amusing moniker came about as a result of the numerous cakes that I make to celebrate birthdays of family and friends. Malia waits impatiently for me to bring out the cake at our gatherings, and then gets excited during our rousing renditions of "Happy Birthday."

Among my happiest cooking experiences have been these birthday cakes. For years I've baked the cake for my nephew Devereux McNair's parties, starting with a vivid green replica of the crocodile from Peter Pan, complete with sharp white chocolate teeth and glowing cherry eyes. Over the years I've concocted a towering clown hat divided into six panels of brightly colored sugars and topped with an explosion of curling ribbons, a shimmering figure eight in silver and white for a skating-rink party, and parallel chocolate loaves that formed a giant eleven, garnished with acrobatic clown figures carrying colorful birthday greeting banners, for a trapeze and trampoline party at a circus school. Now I'm also enjoying baking similar fantasy-theme cakes for my younger nephew Ryan Richardson.

For adult parties, I've created several new cakes that appear in this collection, including Passion Fruit Cake, Fresh Ginger Cake, and Hawaiian Coconut Cake. For a significant February birthday of my sister, Martha McNair, I baked a sophisticated version of a doll cake she had once enjoyed as a little girl. This time the hoopskirt-shaped Velvet Cake was tinted deep purple and covered in amethyst-hued frosting around a grown-up doll outfitted with the contemporary short haircut, bright red lips, and dangling earrings favored by Martha.

While cakes always star at birthday parties, wedding receptions, and other special events, any cake can be cause for a celebration. A piece of warm gingerbread brightens the bleakest midwinter afternoon, and a towering slice of angel food cake with juicy ripe berries turns a summer picnic into a heavenly feast.

This collection of cake recipes is the result of many years of happy baking, beginning with my earliest cooking attempts in the kitchen of my childhood home, the Baptist parsonage in Jonesville, Louisiana. Updated versions of some of those fondly remembered creations are included here.

When I was barely in my teens, my mother and I watched Mildred Swift bake an unorthodox version of pound cake on her local television show, *Looking at Cooking*. We had to try to duplicate it immediately. While the cake was in the oven, our friend and my piano teacher, Lula Alice Little, stopped by for coffee and small-town gossip. As we sat around the Formica-and-chrome dinette table laughing at Lula Alice's constant barrage of wisecracks, the three of us almost polished off the entire still-warm-from-the-oven cake. Ever since, in our family this cake has been known as Happy Cake. To this day, it never ceases to make happy anyone to whom I serve it.

One day while working on this book, I heard Lula Alice had died. I put a Happy Cake (page 24) in the oven, sat down at my piano, and played some of the hymns that I had so often performed when I was the church organist and she was our music director. Memories of my boyhood home, a good friend, and the taste of the warm cake made me happy once again.

Many miles and years away from our Louisiana hometown, my sister's enormous eyes still sparkle when she recalls my peanut cake. As an after-school treat, I added peanut butter to a batter made from a yellow cake mix. While it baked, Martha and I went down to Mr. Burk's service station on the corner across from the church and bought several bags of salted peanuts. I substituted peanut butter for the butter in a cream cheese frosting, and we chopped those salty nuts and pressed them all over the cake. Martha still declares it the best cake ever! Today I use the peanut butter frosting (I have since replaced the salty fried peanuts with unsalted dry-roasted ones) on chocolate cakes that never fail to please all the youngsters and young-at-heartsters in my extended California family.

Through the years, I've thoroughly enjoyed learning more about cake baking, mostly through experimentation and hands-on experience in my own kitchen. Beginning with my late grandmothers, Olivia Belle Keith and Mary Izetta McNair, and my mother, Lucille McNair, I'm indebted to some great American bakers whose sage advice I've sought personally or gleaned from their writings.

Aptly named *The Cake Bible,* Rose Levy Beranbaum's tome revolutionized sponge cakes and buttercreams for me and gave me new ideas for mixing certain batters. My earlier angel food cakes were not nearly as ethereal until the sage advice of my friend Flo Braker, author of *The Simple Art of Perfect Baking.* I used cake flour more frequently in my baking until another friend, national culinary treasure Marion Cunningham (the contemporary Fannie Farmer), pointed out that it produces more "insipid" flavor and texture than all-purpose flour does. Now I reserve cake flour for chiffon, sponge, and other specialties where a light texture is essential. My chocolate recipes have been greatly refined through books and articles by respected chocolate guru Alice Medrich. Likewise, Julia Child, Craig Claiborne, Emily Luchetti, Nick Malgieri, and Martha Stewart have inspired my work, and food scientists Shirley Corriher and Harold Magee have added to my understanding of the chemistry of baking. My nonprofessional cooking friends, especially Ruth Dosher, Naila Gallagher, and Marian May, have each taught me new things, too, and have generously shared recipes.

*Y*es, I plead guilty to having that "all-American sweet tooth" of which a food reviewer once accused me. Many of my recipes reflect a penchant for old-fashioned richness and sweetness instead of the current fashion among many pastry chefs to make not-very-sweet confections. If you prefer things a bit less sweet, try cutting back a little on the sugar. Just keep in mind that sugar tenderizes and changing the amount alters a recipe's chemistry.

My recipe collection includes several chocolate cakes, because to many people cake and chocolate are synonymous. You'll also discover that I'm partial to cakes with tropical influences, perhaps because my partner, Andrew, hails from Hawaii, but more likely because I've always had a natural affinity with those fruity flavors.

In this book I've attempted to include a cake to fit everyone's fancy, ranging from lighter-than-air Hot-Milk Sponge Cake to intensely rich Molten Chocolate Babycakes. Alongside updated versions of gingerbread, fruitcake that you'll want to keep for yourself, and other old standbys, I've placed new cakes that pay homage to some of my favorite contemporary flavors, including passion fruit, fresh ginger, and Italian *gianduja.* A few of my cakes are time-consuming, special-occasion creations that deserve to be placed on pedestals, while others are quick-and-easy, everyday confections to serve in the kitchen right from the baking pan.

You won't find recipes for cheesecakes in these pages, as they are in a dessert class all their own and perhaps deserve their own book. Likewise, I decided not to include the popular flourless chocolate "cakes," dense confections that resemble a cake only in appearance.

*A*s you look at my photographs, you'll see that this is not a cake-decorating book. There are wonderful books on that subject if you enjoy piping more than I do. My preference leans toward simple finishes that are easy, yet give a cake a festive appearance.

As is the custom in all my books, many of my recipes, particularly those for Pound Cake and Chiffon Cake, include numerous variations that insure many days of baking with a constantly changing palette of flavors. Many other recipes, such as Yellow Cake, White Cake, Devil's Food Cake, and Genoise, can be layered with various fillings and frostings to create a bakery of unique cakes that will become staples in your kitchen.

I hope all your cakes turn out to be happy cakes!

Basics

Before beginning to bake any of the cakes in this book,
I urge you to read through this section carefully.
It contains information that you will need to turn to from
time to time as you make your way through a recipe.

EQUIPMENT

$\mathcal{M}$ost of the utensils and equipment needed for cake baking and presentation are already in a well-stocked kitchen, but here is a list of the things that will turn that space into a small, efficient bakery.

If your regular cookware sources do not carry any of these items, check stores or catalogs that specialize in cake-decorating supplies, gourmet kitchenware, and restaurant equipment.

Bowls. Stock a wide range of sizes, from small for whisking eggs to large for sifting together dry ingredients to even larger for mixing batters. Stainless-steel bowls are ideal for beating batters and egg whites and whipping cream. An unlined copper bowl is good for beating egg whites, in which case there's no need to add cream of tartar. If possible, dedicate a bowl to use only for beating egg whites, as any oily residue can prevent the whites from reaching their optimal volume.

Cake decorating turntable. For slicing cakes into layers and for frosting layer cakes, a revolving pedestal is worth the investment. Choose one with a heavy iron base and a rigid metal turntable. A flat lazy Susan makes an acceptable substitute.

Cake spatula. Purchase a special metal spatula large and rigid enough to hold a cake or a cake layer when moving it from a rack or when stacking layers during filling and frosting. Alternatives include the removable bottom of a tart ring, a rimless baking sheet, a metal pizza peel, and a piece of heavy cardboard.

Candy thermometer. An accurate, high-quality thermometer made for resting inside a saucepan is essential for making syrups, fillings, frostings, and sauces.

Cardboard shapes. A heavy piece of cardboard in the same shape and size as a cake bottom makes decorating and moving finished cakes easier. Purchase a variety of shapes and sizes or cut your own from cardboard sheets or boxes.

Covers. Glass or plastic domes that do not touch the frosting are perfect for covering cakes. Plastic cake carriers or other sealable containers are ideal for storing and transporting cakes.

Electric mixers. If you do a lot of baking, invest in both a heavy-duty stand mixer and a hand mixer for various tasks. If possible, purchase an extra bowl to reserve only for beating egg whites.

Folding utensils. Choose a large rounded balloon whisk, a large rubber spatula, or an old-fashioned English angel-cake whisk, a device specifically designed for folding that looks like a miniature metal tennis racket.

Food processor. This is a handy device for finely grinding nuts.

Frosting spatulas. You'll need a large spatula with a flexible metal offset blade for spreading fillings and frosting tops of cakes and a smaller straight-bladed one for frosting sides and loosening cakes from their pans.

Kitchen parchment. This nonstick paper is great for lining pans and other tasks. Purchase rolls or buy flat sheets in bulk. Less expensive waxed paper is an acceptable substitute.

Kitchen scale. Select a reliable scale designed specifically for kitchen use to weigh out bulk chocolate and other ingredients.

Measuring cups and spoons. Proper measuring requires a set of metal or plastic containers in increments from $\frac{1}{4}$ cup to 1 cup for measuring dry ingredients, several glass or plastic cups with vertical marks indicated on the side and a pouring lip for measuring liquids, and a set of metal or plastic measuring spoons in increments from $\frac{1}{4}$ teaspoon to 1 tablespoon.

Oven thermometer. Place this special device in your oven periodically to check for temperature accuracy.

Pans. Heavy-duty aluminum pans with a dull finish are preferable because they conduct heat quickly and evenly. They are a worthwhile investment if you want a great cake. Shiny stainless-steel pans reflect heat and are thus not good conductors, so I don't recommend them. Dark metal pans (including nonstick) and glass pans absorb heat too quickly, which can cause cake edges to overbrown before the center is done. If you must use the latter two types, reduce the oven temperature by 25 degrees.

If the sides of your cakes brown too much or rise faster than the center, purchase insulated pans that provide a cushion of air around the sides, or wrap the exterior of a pan with moistened reusable strips made of aluminized fabric, marketed as Bake-Even or Magic Cake Strips. Both methods keep the pan sides cooler, resulting in a cake with a level surface.

Pastry bags and decorating tips. If you wish to create fancy finishes, choose from a wide variety of bags and tips sold in cake-decorating stores.

Pastry brushes. Earmark a medium-sized brush for greasing pans, stock a large one for whisking away crumbs before frosting, and keep a small one on hand for brushing moistening syrups onto cakes.

Rubber spatulas. Stock up on these handy tools in assorted sizes for scraping bowls, folding flour into batters, and smoothing tops before baking.

Scissors. Keep handy a pair of sharp paper-cutting scissors for turning out parchment liners for pans.

Serrated knife. Bread knives or even longer versions made especially for cakes are ideal for cutting cakes into thinner layers, as well as for serving angel food and other sponge cakes.

Strainers. For sifting dry ingredients, choose a large strainer with medium-sized wire or plastic mesh, a handle, and prongs for resting on the edge of a bowl. You will also need a smaller strainer with finer mesh for straining fillings and sauces. If you prefer using a conventional sifter, choose a heavy-duty one; if it has a triple screen, you will need to sift ingredients together only once.

Texturing combs. Plastic or metal devices with grooves of various widths are useful for adding lines and texture to frostings on a cake.

Wire cake tester. Although this special device composed of a thin rigid wire attached to a plastic holder is not as good for testing cakes as a wooden skewer, it is excellent for loosening cakes from the hollow center tubes of angel food and other tube pans.

Wire racks. Purchase several heavy metal cooling racks that are only a little larger than cake pans. You'll need one for turning out a cake or a layer and another on which to invert each layer.

Wooden skewers. Inserting a slender bamboo skewer into a cake is the best way to test for doneness. Toothpicks can be substituted but are not always long enough to reach the center of loaf and tube cakes.

INGREDIENTS

*B*efore you start to make a cake, measure all the ingredients, bring to room temperature those that call for it, and assemble all the elements on the work space. You do not want to experience any interruptions before you put the cake in the oven.

Flour. Cake flour is finely milled from soft red winter wheat, which has less protein than other types of wheat. During mixing, it develops less gluten to produce a particularly tender cake, making it ideal for angel food, chiffon, and sponge cakes where delicate structure and fine texture are desirable. Cake flour is also heavily bleached, which helps break down the gluten, allows better moisture retention, distributes the fat, and results in a whiter appearance. When purchasing cake flour, usually sold in boxes near the cake mixes and bags of flour, be sure to select plain cake flour, *not* the self-rising type.

For cakes that benefit from a denser structure and heartier flavor, all-purpose flour, a blend of soft and hard red winter wheat, is preferred. Never use high-gluten bread flour for cakes.

To store any flour, transfer it from the package to a canister or other container with a large mouth and a tightly fitting cover.

Leavening. Both baking soda and baking powder help cakes rise by producing carbon dioxide bubbles. They are used on their own or together, depending on the amount of acidity in the batter. Baking soda (sodium bicarbonate) requires the presence of an acidic ingredient such as a soured or cultured milk product to activate it; in the process it neutralizes the tangy flavor of that ingredient. Baking powder, which contains sodium bicarbonate and acid salts as activants, is double-acting, releasing carbon dioxide both from the addition of moisture during mixing and from the heat during baking.

Once baking powder is opened and exposed to moisture in the air, the acid and alkaline ingredients begin to react and it gradually loses its potency. Be sure to write the date on the can when you first open it, and store, tightly covered, in a dry place for up to 6 months. Baking soda may be stored indefinitely in a dry place.

Butter. My fat of choice for cakes is unsalted butter because of its wonderful fresh flavor. Unsalted butter also contains less moisture than salted butter and allows the baker control over how much salt is added. If you make cakes frequently, keep plenty of butter on hand. Unsalted butter turns rancid rather quickly, however, so refrigerate only what you will use within a short time and store extra butter in the freezer for up to several months.

In a few recipes, a little solid vegetable shortening is added along with the butter for moistness. My old practice of making carrot and a few other cakes with vegetable oil, a carryover from my hippie "health-food" days, has been cast aside in favor of using more flavorful melted butter. After several tests with butter and a combination of butter and oil, I still prefer vegetable oil to provide moistness in the old-fashioned Heirloom Apple Cake.

Sugar. Unless specified otherwise, use granulated white sugar whenever recipes call for sugar. Brown sugar is light or dark, depending on the amount of molasses removed during refining that is added back to refined sugar. Powdered sugar, also called confectioners' or icing sugar, is an extremely fine grind of sugar blended with cornstarch to absorb moisture from the air. All sugar should be stored in airtight containers, preferably widemouthed ones for easy scooping.

Eggs. My recipes are written for "large" eggs. Use the freshest eggs possible for optimum volume during beating. Egg whites can be saved from recipes that call for just the yolks and refrigerated for up to 1 week or frozen for up to 1 year, a great way to accumulate the high quantity of whites needed for angel food cakes. To save extra yolks for cakes and curds, tightly cover unbroken yolks and refrigerate for up to 2 days, or blend each yolk with $\frac{1}{2}$ teaspoon sugar to prevent congealing and freeze for up to 2 months.

Dairy products. Although it is possible to use reduced-fat (2 percent) or even low-fat (1 percent) milk in cake batters, the higher fat (about 4 percent) in whole, or homogenized, milk yields a more luxurious cake. I find using fat-free milk unacceptable in cakes.

Buttermilk, which contains only 1.5 percent to 2 percent butterfat and is cultured by the addition of lactic acid bacteria to reduced-fat milk, gives a delightful tang to cakes. It may be used interchangeably in recipes with cultured plain yogurt or sour cream. Avoid fat-free versions with added stabilizers that can separate during baking.

The amount of fat in cream is important in frostings and other finishings. Cream labeled heavy whipping cream contains 36 to 40 percent butterfat, while cream labeled whipping cream contains 30 percent to 36 percent butterfat. Both can be whipped, but heavy cream whips quicker, easier, and lighter and offers more of that old-fashioned flavor. Ultrapasteurized, or sterilized, cream tastes blander than cream not subjected to the treatment. Light cream contains 18 percent to 30 percent butterfat but is rarely sold. In its place I use half-and-half, which is a dairy blend of equal parts light cream and milk and contains at least 10.5 percent butterfat. Do not substitute milk for these products unless listed as an alternative.

I enjoy the rich caramellike flavor imparted by canned evaporated milk in certain recipes. Don't confuse evaporated milk with sweetened condensed milk, an intensely sweet and thickened canned product used in some toppings.

Chocolate. Unsweetened chocolate, or chocolate liquor, contains only cocoa solids and cocoa butter gleaned from roasted cocoa beans and is too bitter for eating out of hand. Extra cocoa butter, sugar, vanilla, and perhaps lecithin are added to create bittersweet or semisweet chocolate. Milk solids, butter, and vanilla are added to arrive at milk chocolate, which is rarely used in baking cakes but does make a mild alternative to the more robust flavors of bittersweet and semisweet chocolates in frostings. White chocolate contains cocoa butter and no cocoa solids. Always use the finest-quality chocolate you can locate and afford. Store unsweetened, bittersweet, and semisweet chocolate well wrapped in a cool, dry place for up to 1 year. Purchase milk chocolate and white chocolate when you plan to use them.

Cocoa. Unsweetened chocolate liquor that has had most of the cocoa butter removed is ground to a powder to make cocoa. Natural cocoa imparts a strong chocolate flavor and is slightly acidic; baking soda is often used in combination with it to neutralize the acid. Alkalized cocoa, usually labeled Dutch-processed, has been neutralized for a milder, less acidic flavor. I usually prefer natural unsweetened cocoa in cake batters and alkalized cocoa in frostings, but feel free to use them interchangeably according to preference. Store airtight in a cool, dry place indefinitely.

Extracts. Blind tastings held by major food publications indicate that panelists cannot detect the difference in sweets baked with pure vanilla extract versus imitation vanilla flavoring. In uncooked frostings and toppings, however, imitation vanilla imparts a bitter taste. I prefer to use the real thing every time.

I also prefer pure extracts of other flavorings. Intense imported essences and concentrated oils in a wide range of flavors are available from cake-decorating supply stores and should be added cautiously a few drops at a time.

Zests. Use only the outer colored portion of lemon or other citrus peel, leaving the bitter white pith behind. When a recipe calls for grated or minced fresh zest, I prefer to remove the zest with a citrus zester that renders long shreds, then finely chop the shreds with a knife. If using a grater, be careful not to bear down hard enough to go into the pith.

MEASUREMENTS

Always use the correct type of measuring device (see page 9).

To measure flour, first stir it in its storage container with a fork or spoon or shake the container a few times. This will aerate it. Select a metal or plastic cup made specifically for measuring dry ingredients in the exact increment being measured. Lightly spoon the flour from the container into the measuring cup and fill to overflowing; avoid packing the flour down or shaking the cup. Using a straight edge such as the back of a knife, a metal spatula, or a dough scraper, sweep off the excess to level the flour even with the top of the measuring cup. Some bakers prefer to dip the measuring cup into the flour and scoop to fill to overflowing, then sweep off the excess. Although the weight will vary slightly between the two methods, either way is accurate enough for most cakes.

Professional bakers rely on weighing flour. If you wish to weigh instead of measuring, use a reliable kitchen scale. The spoon-and-level measuring method used for all of the recipes in this book normally yields 121 grams or 4.25 ounces per cup of all-purpose flour and 114 grams or 4 ounces per cup of cake flour. The dip-and-level method yields 145 grams or 5 ounces per cup of all-purpose flour and 130 grams or 4.5 ounces of cake flour.

To measure baking powder, baking soda, salt, and spices, fill the appropriate-sized measuring spoon and level off the top with a straight edge such as a spatula.

To measure milk and other liquids, set a clear measuring cup on a level surface and pour in liquid until it reaches the desired mark. For accuracy, view the cup at eye level to be certain that the liquid is even with the appropriate mark.

TEMPERATURE

*C*old butter, eggs, and milk or milk products added to other cake batter ingredients will not blend well and will cause the mixture to separate. Be sure to remove these items from the refrigerator or freezer in time for them to come to normal room temperature, or about 70° F, before adding them.

Butter should be pliable yet still firm. If it becomes too soft, the air cells will break and the butter will be unable to trap air during beating. Unwrap cold butter, cut it into small pieces, and set it on the wrapper near the mixer to come to room temperature.

Crack cold eggs into a glass measuring cup with a pouring lip, beat them lightly, and let them come to room temperature. This step speeds up the warming, and the beaten eggs are ready to be drizzled into the batter. (The old-fashioned method of cracking one egg at a time into a batter followed by beating well can result in overbeating, which breaks the emulsion of the batter.) When recipes call for separated eggs, for ease, divide the eggs into yolks and whites when cold, then bring to room temperature before using.

Pour cold milk or milk products directly into a measuring cup so they are ready to use when warmed up.

When you think the ingredients have warmed to the right temperature, insert an instant-read thermometer into several pieces of the butter, the eggs, and the milk to be certain that your hunch was correct.

Should you forget to remove ingredients from the refrigerator or freezer ahead of time or merely wish to speed up the process, here are a few shortcuts. Unwrap and cut up butter, crack or separate eggs, or measure milk as suggested above. Place in a microwave oven and run at a low setting, stopping and checking every 10 seconds, until warmed to room temperature. Do not let the butter begin to melt, the eggs begin to cook, or the milk get too warm. Eggs or milk can also be placed in measuring cups and set in bowls of warm water until they reach room temperature.

CHOOSING AND PREPARING PANS

*T*he baking times and the texture of a finished cake will vary with the depth of the batter. Normally, the thinner the batter is spread, the lighter the final texture, but the cake must be watched carefully to prevent overbaking or it will be dry. I like moist cakes with velvety textures, so I prefer to bake thicker cakes or layers, then split the cooled layers when more are desired.

Whenever possible, use the size and type of pan called for in a recipe. Pans that are too large can overheat the rim of the cake and result in mounds or cracks. Pans that are too small result in batter overflowing the rim and producing terrible oven messes.

Following is a list of the pans called for in my recipes with their approximate full-capacity volumes; pan measurements are taken across the top of the pan and may vary slightly according to the manufacturer.

9-by-5-inch loaf pan: 8 cups

9-by-2-inch round cake pan: 9 cups

9-by-2-inch square pan: 10 cups

9-inch springform pan: 12 cups

10-inch Bundt or other fluted tube pan: 12 cups

10-inch angel food or other straight-sided tube pan: 14 cups

13-by-9-inch pan: 15 cups

17-by-12-inch jelly-roll or half-sheet pan: 12 cups

If you must substitute a pan or wish a different shape or size, choose one of similar capacity. Measure the amount of water that will fill that pan to the rim and find a pan on the list that holds the same quantity. A batter can also be divided among two or more pans that add up to the same capacity, or placed in a single larger pan instead of multiple layer pans.

Until you have baked a specific batter in a particular pan to know how high it will rise, it is a good idea to fill any pan no more than two-thirds full. (If you have a little extra batter, make an individual cake as a cook's reward.) An exception to this rule is fruitcake, where you'll be instructed to fill the pan fully, as it rises little during the slow baking.

For decades I greased and floured pans to keep cakes from sticking. Now I simply grease the pan and line the bottom with kitchen parchment (see page 8). With this method the bottom of a cake never sticks to the pan and there is no flour mess to clean up. Perhaps best of all, less crust forms on the bottom and sides of the cake. Exceptions to this method are fluted or decorative pans with curves, nooks, and crannies that cannot be lined with paper.

Even pans with nonstick finishes should be greased and lined or greased and floured for easy release. Avoid using nonstick pans for angel food and chiffon cakes, which must hang upside down in their pans until cooled.

Solid vegetable shortening works best for greasing because it is flavorless and coats evenly. If you object to the use of this hydrogenated shortening in cooking, you can substitute butter, but keep in mind that butter can leave ungreased gaps as it melts and can burn or overbrown the crust of the cake. I prefer using a brush to apply the shortening generously for a more uniform coating, especially for getting into surfaces of fluted or decorative pans. Spreading with a piece of waxed paper is an alternative used by many bakers, but the coating is not as even. Although some bakers enjoy the convenience of vegetable oil cooking sprays or aerosol products that contain both oil and flour, I find that sprays tend to glob unevenly on pan surfaces.

To grease and line a pan, using a pastry brush, lightly grease the bottom and sides of the pan with room-temperature solid shortening. (Some of my recipes, such as those for angel food and chiffon cakes, will direct you not to grease the sides of the pan, as the batter needs the ungreased surface to climb.) Place the pan on a sheet of kitchen parchment and trace around the bottom of the pan with a pencil, then cut out the traced shape with a pair of scissors. Lay the parchment in the pan and use your hand to smooth out any wrinkles. If desired, lightly brush the paper with more solid shortening for easy removal of the paper after baking.

To grease and line a jelly-roll pan, using a pastry brush, lightly grease only the bottom of the pan with room-temperature solid shortening; do not grease the sides. Cut a piece of kitchen parchment wide enough to cover the bottom of the pan completely and long enough to overhang the edges on the two opposite short ends by about 2 inches. If desired, lightly brush the paper with more solid shortening for easy removal of the paper after baking.

To grease and flour a pan, using a pastry brush, generously grease the bottom and sides of the pan with room-temperature solid shortening; be sure to coat every nook and cranny of fluted or decorative pans. Sprinkle generously with all-purpose flour, tilt and rotate the pan to coat all greased surfaces with flour, invert the pan over a sink, and tap the bottom of the pan or rap it against the edge of the sink to remove excess flour. For chocolate cakes, in a small bowl, combine three parts flour with one part unsweetened cocoa, stir well, and use in place of the flour.

To grease a pan for a cake that will be served directly from the pan, using a pastry brush, generously grease the bottom and sides of the pan with room-temperature solid shortening. Do not line with parchment or dust with flour.

When baking angel food and chiffon cakes, do not grease the pan, line with parchment, or dust with flour. The egg white mixture needs the ungreased sides of the pan to climb during rising and the ungreased bottom to hang onto while cooling upside down in the pan.

PREPARING AN OVEN

While readying ingredients and pans, prepare an oven for baking. Unless otherwise directed in recipes, position racks so that the cake will bake in the middle of the oven for even heat distribution. Preheat the oven to the temperature given in individual recipes; 350° F is ideal for most cakes.

Be certain that your oven temperature is accurate. When too hot, the sides of a cake will set before the middle does, resulting in humps or cracks. When the oven is too cold, it allows air to escape from the air cells in the rising batter before it has a chance to set, resulting in sunken centers and coarse textures. Purchase an oven thermometer that can be placed inside the oven to check for accuracy. If the oven temperature does not match the oven setting dial, adjust the setting as needed to maintain the correct baking temperature.

MIXING BATTER

The goal in mixing cake batter is a well-blended emulsion with evenly distributed ingredients surrounded by tiny air bubbles. Each ingredient must be beaten or folded into the mixture in proper sequence to create and preserve the prized emulsion.

To ready dry ingredients, combine the flour and other dry ingredients as directed in recipes. For most cakes, I recommend sifting the dry ingredients together to aerate and lighten them for easier mixing. For a particularly light mixture, I call for sifting two more times. You can use a traditional sifter, but I prefer sifting through a mesh strainer (see page 9) into a bowl, shaking the strainer and using a small whisk or a cooking spoon to hasten ingredients through the mesh and to break up any remaining lumps. The strainer is easier to use and clean than a sifter. Many bakers advocate sifting onto a sheet of kitchen parchment or waxed paper, but I find that some ingredients can be lost along the edges of the paper during sifting or transferring and prefer confining the dry ingredients in bowls.

After the final sifting, whisk the dry ingredients to blend them thoroughly before they are added to the batter, where they will only be briefly stirred or lightly folded into the emulsion.

To mix ingredients, carefully follow the detailed directions in each recipe, as different types of cakes require specific methods.

I urge you to invest in a heavy-duty stand mixer or a powerful hand mixer, or preferably both for various tasks. While it is certainly possible to make good cakes with whisks and spoons, these modern machines make the process easier and produce consistently perfect batters.

When folding ingredients, use a large bowl that provides plenty of room for the process. Use a mixer set on low speed or a rubber spatula to fold dry ingredients into most batters. When folding foam or sponge cake batters, choose a large balloon whisk, large rubber spatula, or English angel-cake whisk (see page 8). When folding dry ingredients into beaten egg white mixtures, I usually start with a balloon whisk to incorporate the first batch or two of flour, then switch to an English angel-cake whisk to fold the remaining additions. At the very end, I use a rubber spatula to be certain that none of the flour mixture has fallen to the bottom of the bowl and to transfer the batter to the pan.

Whether folding dry ingredients or beaten egg whites into a batter, always add the lighter mixture on top of the heavier mixture. If you are not using a mixer, push the folding utensil down through the center of the two mixtures to the bottom of the bowl. Using your wrist, scrape the utensil across the bottom of the bowl, then pull it up the side and over the top of the mixtures. As the utensil comes over the top, using your free hand, give the bowl a quarter turn. Working as quickly yet as gently as possible, repeat this process just until the ingredients are well blended. Avoid overfolding, which deflates the batter.

When beating egg whites, for maximum volume, use a metal bowl and beaters that are immaculately clean and free of all traces of fat. (It is virtually impossible to wash away all traces of fat from plastic bowls.) If there is any doubt about oily residue, wipe out a well-washed bowl with vinegar and rub completely dry with paper toweling. If you use a traditional unlined copper mixing bowl, omit the cream of tartar called for in recipes.

BAKING AND COOLING

As soon as the batter is mixed, hold the bowl over a prepared pan and use a rubber spatula or spoon to scrape the batter into the pan. When using multiple pans, divide the batter as evenly as possible; I usually just add a little at a time to each pan until they appear even. If perfectly symmetrical layers are important to you, weigh each pan on a kitchen scale and spoon batter from one to another to equalize weight.

Transfer the pan(s) to the preheated oven. For optimal heat distribution and even baking, place the pans at least 3 inches from the oven walls and at least 3 inches apart.

Bake until the cake tests done as directed in recipes; start to check for doneness several minutes before the shortest specified time.

While the cake is baking, place a sturdy metal rack or racks on a work surface. When the cake tests done, remove the pan(s) from the oven and place on the rack(s) to cool as specified in recipes.

Angel food and chiffon cakes must be completely cooled with their pans turned upside down. Most modern tube pans have extended prongs on top on which to rest the upside-down pan. Even with this convenience, I prefer to turn the pan upside down and place the hollow tube of the pan over a long-necked bottle or metal funnel. This keeps the bottom of the pan in place and prevents it from coming loose and crushing a section of the cake during cooling. If baked in a springform pan, rest the rim of the pan on 3 or 4 same-sized glasses evenly spaced around the perimeter of the pan. It normally takes $1\frac{1}{2}$ to 2 hours for these cakes to cool completely.

REMOVING

$\mathcal{T}$he best way to invert cakes from the pans is with wire racks (see page 10). I use a large rack to cool cakes in their pans, then a pair of smaller racks slightly larger than the cake pans for turning out.

To remove a warm cake from the pan, after cooling briefly as directed, carefully insert the blade of a thin, flexible metal spatula or knife between the cake and the pan wall, then pressing against the pan to prevent cutting the sides of the cake, slowly run the blade all the way around the circumference of the pan to loosen the cake from the pan edges. If baked in a springform pan, unclasp and remove the ring. Invert a lightly greased wire rack over the cake, invert the rack and pan or springform bottom together, and lift off the pan or springform bottom. Peel off the parchment, if using. If the cake needs to be inverted again so it is top side up, place another lightly greased rack over the cake and invert. Set aside on the rack to cool further as directed in recipes before finishing or serving.

To remove a cooled cake from the pan, let the cake cool completely, then proceed as for removing a warm cake, above. After turning out the cake onto a rack and peeling off the parchment, the cake can be inverted directly onto a serving plate.

To remove an angel food or chiffon cake from the pan, after cooling completely as directed, turn the pan upright and place on a work surface. Carefully insert the blade of a thin, flexible metal spatula or knife between the cake and the pan wall, then pressing against the pan to prevent cutting the sides of the cake, slowly run the blade all the way around the circumference of the pan to loosen the cake from the pan edges. Using a wire cake tester or a small spatula or knife, repeat this procedure around the hollow tube. Holding one side of the pan with one hand, push up the removable bottom with your other hand to lift and remove the cake from the ring portion. Holding the hollow tube with one hand, tilt the cake on its side on a work surface, then rotate and tap all around the edge of the pan bottom until the cake is loosened from the bottom. If necessary, run the blade of the metal spatula between the cake and the pan bottom to loosen completely. Invert a lightly greased wire rack or a serving plate over the cake, invert the rack or plate and pan bottom together, and lift off the pan bottom.

FINISHING

$\mathcal{O}$nce a cake or layers are cooled (or while cooling, depending on the recipe), prepare the glaze or filling and/or frosting as directed. Be ready to work with it as soon as it reaches the correct pourable or spreadable consistency; some require quick work before they harden, while others allow for a more leisurely pace.

Whenever you need to move a cake or layer for finishing or decorating, use a rigid rimless surface that is wide enough to hold the cake or layer, such as a cake spatula (see page 8). Slip it under the cake layer and lift it.

To glaze a cake, place the cake on a wire rack and set on a baking sheet to catch any excess glaze that can be used again. Quickly pour or spoon the glaze onto the center of the cake, or around the top if a tube cake, then lift the rack and gently rock the cake to coat the top completely and allow excess glaze to run down the sides. If coating with a thick glaze, you may need to use a long metal frosting spatula to spread the glaze in a thin even layer across the top and to push excess glaze down over the sides. For a smooth finish, avoid making marks in the glaze. If you wish to coat the sides completely, use the spatula to spread the glaze thinly before it has a chance to set up. Let stand or refrigerate undisturbed on the rack until the glaze is set.

To slice a cake into layers (or to slice thick layers into thinner layers), using a long serrated knife, first trim off any humps to even the top of the cake or each layer.

Place the cake or layer on a cake decorating turntable (see page 8) or a flat lazy Susan. Position a long serrated knife in the center of the side of the cake or layer (or where you wish the slice to occur if making more than 2 layers). While holding the knife in a steady position with one hand, place your other hand on top of the cake and turn the cake to cut a groove into it all the way around. Continuing to turn the cake, gradually cut horizontally from the groove into the center to slice all the way through the cake.

Alternatively, place the cake on a work surface. Place one of your hands on top of the cake to steady it. Position a long serrated knife in the center of the side of the cake or layer (or where you wish the slice to occur if making more than 2 layers). Slowly cut horizontally all the way through the cake, maintaining as straight a line as possible.

Insert a toothpick into the same position of each layer to create a vertical line of markers that will be helpful in reassembling the layers when filling the cake. Transfer each layer to a work surface or plate.

To soak a cake or layers with soaking syrup, using a small, sharp knife and your fingertips, scrape and pull off the crust from the top and bottom of the cake or each layer so the syrup can penetrate. Transfer the cake or a layer to a sheet of plastic wrap. Using a small bulb baster or a spoon, evenly drizzle enough soaking liquid onto the cake or layer to moisten it completely. Cover with a second sheet of plastic wrap and carefully invert the cake or layer. Pull off the top sheet of plastic wrap and moisten the top with soaking liquid in the same manner. Repeat the process with any remaining layers.

When filling and/or frosting a cake, choose a serving plate or cake pedestal large enough to hold the cake. For easier and more elaborate decorating, a cake decorating turntable (see page 8) is a valuable addition to the kitchen. As it is often difficult to transfer a finished cake from a decorating turntable to a serving plate or pedestal, consider placing the first layer on a piece of cardboard the same size and shape as the cake (see page 8). To anchor a cake to a cardboard base, spoon a dollop of frosting in the center of the cardboard before adding the first layer.

To fill a layer cake, using a pastry brush, lightly brush away any stray crumbs from the top and sides of all of the layers. Place a layer, bottom side down, in the center of the serving plate or cake pedestal or on the decorating turntable. If working on a serving plate or pedestal, slip strips of kitchen parchment or waxed paper underneath the edge of the layer all the way around to keep the plate or pedestal clean.

Spoon some of the filling (or frosting) onto the layer and spread evenly with a long metal frosting spatula. Place another layer on top; if using split layers, use the top half and line up the toothpicks to achieve evenness. Spread filling and continue to add any remaining layers in the same manner until all layers have been used.

If a soft filling causes the layers to begin to slide, quickly transfer the cake to a refrigerator or freezer for a few minutes, just until set enough to hold together before continuing with filling.

To frost a cake, using a pastry brush, lightly brush away any visible stray crumbs from the top or sides. Using a long metal frosting spatula, spread a thin layer of frosting over the sides and top of the cake, using just enough to secure any loose crumbs and fill in any cracks or crevices. If crumbs adhere to your spatula during spreading, scrape the spatula clean before dipping it back into the bowl of frosting. Scoop some of the remaining frosting on top of the cake and spread evenly, then scoop and spread the remaining frosting, a little at a time, onto the sides of the cake to coat evenly.

If you wish to create texture, use a cake decorating comb to create ridges or use the spatula or a spoon to create swirls or peaks. For a very smooth finish, go over the cake with an offset metal frosting spatula.

To decorate with frosting, spoon the remaining frosting or a compatible frosting or whipped cream into a pastry bag fitted with a decorative tip. Holding the tip end of the bag with one hand, twist the open end of the bag with your other hand until the frosting just begins to flow out of the tip. Pipe desired shapes around the cake base or perimeter of the cake top, or as desired.

If necessary, or advised in a recipe, refrigerate the completed cake, uncovered, until the frosting is firm.

GARNISHING

There are numerous wonderful books on fanciful cake decorating if you wish to create elaborate designs. My preference is for simplicity.

Nothing looks better on a cake than a few perfect fresh flowers or a shower of fragrant rose petals. Chocolate leaves and other decorative shapes (see page 126) always add a festive note, as does a simple sprinkling of colorful edible confetti or a dusting of powdered sugar or cocoa, done with or without a stencil. You'll see ideas for other finishing touches throughout my photographs.

STORING

Most cakes should be served as soon as possible after they are finished, although a few benefit from "aging," which I've indicated in recipes. When you need to store a frosted cake, cover it with a dome or place it in a sealable plastic cake container. Tightly wrap a pound cake or other unfrosted cake in plastic wrap.

Store cakes without frostings or fillings or those finished with powdered sugar or cooked egg-white frostings or fillings at room temperature for up to 2 days. Refrigerate cakes filled and frosted with mixtures made from butter, cream, and other dairy products for up to 2 days.

When choosing a frosting, keep in mind that the texture of foam or sponge cakes holds up well during refrigeration, while butter cakes dry out quickly.

If you need to work ahead, tightly wrap cake layers in plastic wrap, then in aluminum foil, and store at room temperature for up to 2 days or freeze for up to several weeks prior to frosting.

Although most frosted cakes can be frozen, some frostings and glazes will crack. To freeze, wrap a cake tightly in plastic wrap, then in aluminum foil and freeze for up to several weeks; thaw in a refrigerator or at room temperature.

All chilled cakes taste best when brought to room temperature before serving.

HIGH-ALTITUDE BAKING

When I'm in residence at my Lake Tahoe home, which is at 6,250 feet above sea level, I most often choose to make desserts other than cakes. But by making a few adjustments to my recipes, which are developed and tested in my almost-at-sea-level San Francisco home, I've baked excellent pound cakes, gingerbreads, devil's food cakes, and other butter cakes in the mountains.

The reduced air pressure at altitudes over 3,000 feet creates numerous complications with cake baking. Liquids boil at a lower temperature, which means they evaporate more quickly. The result can be a dry cake or weakened structure. Leavenings cause more expansion, which can lead to a collapsed cake before starch cells have a chance to set. Sugar becomes more concentrated, and too much sugar may prevent the cake from setting.

Unfortunately, there are no definite rules to insure success at every altitude, but the following general guidelines, based on recommendations of the USDA and food scientists, should prove helpful. Always make notes in recipe margins and keep experimenting until you reach the right formula for your locale. You may experience a few flops, but once you get it right, you can modify recipes for a lifetime of great cakes.

At any elevation over 3,000 feet above sea level, increase the oven temperature by 25 degrees for faster setting and better texture. When baking pound cakes that use no or very little chemical leavening, reduce each $\frac{1}{2}$ cup (1 stick) butter by 1 to 2 tablespoons to strengthen the structure of the cake. When baking angel food and other sponge-type recipes that call for beaten egg whites instead of chemical leaveners, beat the whites only until they form soft peaks, not the usual stiff peaks, and either reduce the amount of sugar as suggested below or add a bit of extra flour.

At 3,000 to 5,000 feet above sea level, reduce each teaspoon of baking powder or baking soda by $\frac{1}{8}$ teaspoon, reduce each cup of sugar by 1 tablespoon, and increase each cup of liquid by 2 tablespoons.

At 5,000 to 7,000 feet above sea level, reduce each teaspoon of baking powder or baking soda by $\frac{1}{8}$ to $\frac{1}{4}$ teaspoon, reduce each cup of sugar by 2 tablespoons, and increase each cup of liquid by 2 to 3 tablespoons.

At 7,000 to 10,000 feet above sea level, reduce each teaspoon of baking powder or baking soda by $\frac{1}{4}$ to $\frac{1}{2}$ teaspoon, reduce each cup of sugar by 2 to 3 tablespoons, and increase each cup of liquid by 3 to 4 tablespoons.

At over 10,000 feet above sea level, increase each cup of flour by 1 to 2 tablespoons, reduce each teaspoon of baking powder or baking soda by $\frac{1}{4}$ to $\frac{1}{2}$ teaspoon, reduce each cup of sugar by 2 to 3 tablespoons, add 1 extra egg, and increase each cup of liquid by 3 to 4 tablespoons.

Cakes

Following are cakes for any day of the week, as well as for very special occasions. Some are delectable right from the oven, yet others need the suggested fillings and frostings. In addition to several unique cakes, I've included beloved classics such as sponge cake and white cake that are indispensable components of other cakes. Space constraints require the inclusion of many referrals to other pages for details. But once you've mastered the basics of cake baking described in the previous pages, you'll rarely need to look back at those directions.

Pound Cake

Early recipes for this classic literally called for a pound each of flour, butter, sugar, and eggs. This contemporary version weighs in a bit lighter but equally delicious. For a large pound cake, double the recipe and bake in a 10-inch angel food or other straight tube pan for about 1^1/$_2$ hours. ❄ Although it is difficult to beat the rich buttery flavor of a plain pound cake, I've given a few scrumptious variations.

MAKES 10 SERVINGS.

Position racks so that the cake will bake in the middle of an oven and preheat the oven to 325° F. Grease and line a 9-by-5-inch loaf pan as directed on page 14. Set aside.

Place the flour and salt together in a strainer or sifter and sift into a bowl. Whisk to mix well and set aside.

In the bowl of a stand mixer fitted with a flat beater, or in a bowl with a hand mixer, beat the butter at medium speed until soft and creamy, about 45 seconds. With the mixer still running, slowly add the sugar, then stop the mixer and scrape the mixture that clings to the sides of the bowl into the center. Continue beating at medium speed until very light and fluffy, about 5 minutes. Slowly drizzle in the eggs and egg yolks and beat well; stop at least once to scrape the sides of the bowl. Add the vanilla and blend well.

Using the mixer on low speed or a rubber spatula, fold in about one-third of the flour mixture, scraping the sides of the bowl and folding just until the flour mixture is incorporated. In the same manner, fold in half of the remaining flour mixture, and finally the remaining flour mixture.

Scrape the batter into the prepared pan and smooth the surface with a rubber spatula. Bake until the cake springs back when lightly touched in the center with your fingertip and a wooden skewer inserted into the center of the cake comes out clean, 1 hour to 1$\frac{1}{4}$ hours.

Remove the pan to a wire rack to cool for 5 to 10 minutes, then turn the cake out onto the rack to cool completely as directed on page 17.

1^3/$_4$ cups all-purpose flour

^{1}/$_2$ teaspoon salt

1 cup (2 sticks) unsalted butter, at room temperature

1^1/$_2$ cups sugar

4 eggs, at room temperature, lightly beaten

3 egg yolks, at room temperature, lightly beaten

2 teaspoons pure vanilla extract

variations ➤

Yellow Cake

As American as apple pie and much easier to make, these buttery layers are favorite components of myriad layer cakes.
One of the most popular ways to frost yellow cake is with Chocolate Frosting (page 114), and a shower of confectioner's confetti
from a cake-decorating supply store turns it into a colorful party cake.

MAKES 12 SERVINGS.

$2\frac{1}{2}$ *cups plus 2 tablespoons cake flour*

1 tablespoon baking powder

$\frac{3}{4}$ teaspoon salt

1 cup (2 sticks) unsalted butter, at
room temperature

2 cups sugar

6 egg yolks, at room temperature,
lightly beaten

2 eggs, at room temperature, lightly
beaten

2 teaspoons pure vanilla extract

1 cup buttermilk, at room temperature

Filling and/or frosting (see pages
106–119; optional)

*P*osition racks so that the cake layers will bake in the middle of an oven and preheat the oven to 350° F. Grease and line two 9-inch round cake pans as directed on page 14. Set aside.

Place the flour, baking powder, and salt together in a strainer or sifter and sift into a bowl. Repeat the process two more times. Whisk to mix well and set aside.

In the bowl of a stand mixer fitted with a flat beater, or in a bowl with a hand mixer, beat the butter at medium speed until soft and creamy, about 45 seconds. With the mixer still running, slowly add the sugar, then stop the mixer and scrape the mixture that clings to the sides of the bowl into the center. Continue beating at medium speed until very light and fluffy, about 5 minutes. Slowly drizzle in the egg yolks and eggs and beat well; stop at least once to scrape the sides of the bowl. Add the vanilla and blend well.

Using the mixer on low speed or a rubber spatula, fold in about one-third of the flour mixture, then half of the buttermilk, scraping the sides of the bowl and folding just until the ingredients are incorporated. In the same manner, fold in half of the remaining flour mixture, then the remaining buttermilk, and finally the remaining flour mixture.

Divide the batter evenly between the prepared pans and smooth the surfaces with a rubber spatula. Bake until each cake layer springs back when lightly touched in the center with your fingertip and a wooden skewer inserted into the center of each layer comes out clean, about 30 minutes.

Remove the pans to a wire rack to cool for 5 to 10 minutes, then turn the layers out onto the rack to cool completely as directed on page 17.

Use the layers as directed in other recipes, or prepare a favorite filling and/or frosting and fill and frost the cake as directed on pages 18–19.

VARIATION

Spice Cake

Add 2 teaspoons ground cinnamon, 1 teaspoon ground allspice, $\frac{1}{2}$ teaspoon ground cloves, and $\frac{1}{2}$ teaspoon freshly grated nutmeg to the flour mixture when sifting. Substitute 1 cup firmly packed light brown sugar for 1 cup of the granulated sugar.

White Cake

These tender, downy white layers are compatible with almost any frosting and suitable for any occasion. A dreamy finish for the cake for a wedding or other elegant event is vanilla-flavored Buttercream (page 112) with a garnish of finely chopped pistachio nuts.

MAKES 12 SERVINGS.

¾ cup egg whites (from about 6 eggs), at room temperature

1 cup whole milk, at room temperature

2 teaspoons pure vanilla extract

2½ cups cake flour

2½ teaspoons baking powder

¾ teaspoon salt

1¾ cups sugar

¾ cup (1½ sticks) unsalted butter, at room temperature

Filling and/or frosting (see pages 106–119; optional)

Position racks so that the cake layers will bake in the middle of an oven and preheat the oven to 350° F. Grease and line two 9-inch round cake pans as directed on page 14. Set aside.

In a bowl or glass measuring cup, combine the egg whites, milk, and vanilla and whisk to blend well. Set aside.

Place the flour, baking powder, and salt together in a strainer or sifter and sift into a bowl. Add the sugar and mix with an electric mixer at low speed until well blended, about 30 seconds. Add the butter and beat at medium speed until the mixture resembles coarse bread crumbs, about 45 seconds.

Add about 1¼ cups of the egg white mixture and beat at medium speed if using a stand mixer or high speed if using a hand mixer for 1½ minutes, then stop the mixer and scrape the mixture that clings to the sides of the bowl into the center. Add the remaining egg white mixture and beat at the same speed for 30 seconds, then stop and scrape down the sides of the bowl and beat again until creamy smooth, about 30 seconds.

Divide the batter evenly between the prepared pans and smooth the surfaces with a rubber spatula. Bake until each cake layer springs back when lightly touched in the center with your fingertip and a wooden skewer inserted into the center of each layer comes out clean, about 25 minutes.

Remove the pans to a wire rack to cool for 5 to 10 minutes, then turn the layers out onto the rack to cool completely as directed on page 17.

Use the layers as directed in other recipes, or prepare a favorite filling and/or frosting and fill and frost the cake as directed on pages 18–19.

Genoise

A hallmark of professional bakers, this sponge cake of Italian origin and French perfection has an infinite variety of uses. The dry cake is often split into two layers and always sprinkled with a simple sugar syrup or other liquid before filling and frosting. ❊ For one of my favorite cakes, as shown here, split the cake into two layers, then fill and top with one of the curds on page 108. Spread a thin layer of the curd onto the sides to glaze lightly, and dust the top with powdered sugar.

MAKES 8 SERVINGS.

$\mathcal{P}$osition racks so that the cake will bake in the middle of an oven and preheat the oven to 350° F. Grease and line a 9-inch springform pan as directed on page 14. Set aside.

Place the flour, cornstarch, salt, and 2 tablespoons of the sugar together in a strainer or sifter and sift into a bowl. Repeat the process two more times. Whisk to mix well and set aside.

In the metal bowl of a stand mixer or a metal bowl, lightly whisk together the eggs and the remaining ½ cup sugar. Set the bowl over a pan of simmering water, being sure that the bottom of the bowl doesn't touch the water, and whisk gently just until the mixture is lukewarm to the touch. Remove from the heat. Using the wire whip of a stand mixer or hand mixer, beat the egg mixture at high speed until light, fluffy, at least tripled in bulk, and a wide ribbon forms when some of the mixture is lifted and dropped back over the remainder, about 5 minutes if using a stand mixer, or about 10 minutes if using a hand mixer.

Meanwhile, in a small saucepan, heat the clarified butter just until hot. Pour into a bowl, stir in the vanilla, and cover to keep warm.

Spoon about 1 cup of the egg mixture into the warm butter mixture. Using a small rubber spatula, fold as directed on page 16 to mix well. Set aside.

Sift about one-third of the flour mixture over the remaining egg mixture in the mixing bowl. Using a large balloon whisk or rubber spatula, quickly and gently fold the mixture just until the flour mixture is incorporated. In the same way, quickly and gently fold in the remaining flour mixture in 2 equal batches; the flour must be well incorporated, but avoid overmixing and deflating the batter too much. Finally, fold in the butter mixture just until well incorporated.

Scrape the batter into the prepared pan and smooth the surface with a rubber

½ cup plus 2 tablespoons cake flour
¼ cup cornstarch
½ teaspoon salt
½ cup plus 2 tablespoons sugar
4 eggs
3 tablespoons clarified butter (see Note on page 32)
1 teaspoon pure vanilla extract
Soaking Syrup (page 106; optional)
Filling and/or frosting (see pages 106–119; optional)

recipe continues ➤

about 25 minutes; to prevent falling, do not open the oven door until near the end of the minimum baking time.

Remove the pan to a wire rack to cool completely, then turn the cake out onto a work surface as directed on page 17. Using a small, sharp knife and your fingertips, scrape and pull off the crust from the top and bottom of the cake.

Use the cake as directed in other recipes, or slice horizontally in half as directed on page 18, prepare a favorite filling and/or frosting, and fill and frost the cake as directed on pages 18–19.

VARIATION

Chocolate Sponge Cake

Substitute $^1/_4$ cup unsweetened cocoa for $^1/_4$ cup of the flour.

American Sponge Cake

Our classic sponge cake relies on air beaten into the egg whites for volume and sugar instead of fat for tenderness. ❋ *To make the venerable Boston Cream Pie, shown here, bake the cake in a springform pan, split the cake into two equal layers, and fill with Custard Filling (page 106). Cover the top of the cake only with about 1 cup Ganache (page 117) made with semisweet chocolate and decorate with chocolate leaves (see page 126).*

MAKES 8 SERVINGS.

1 cup cake flour

1 1/2 cups sugar

1/2 teaspoon salt

6 egg yolks, at room temperature

2 teaspoons finely grated or minced
   fresh lemon zest

1 teaspoon pure vanilla extract

1/2 teaspoon pure lemon extract

1 cup egg whites (from about 8 eggs),
   at room temperature

1 teaspoon cream of tartar

Filling and/or frosting (see pages
   106–119; optional)

Position racks so that the cake will bake in the middle of an oven and preheat the oven to 350° F. Select a 10-inch springform pan or a 10-inch angel food or other straight tube pan with a removable bottom; do not grease or line. Set aside.

Place the flour, 1/4 cup of the sugar, and the salt together in a strainer or sifter and sift into a bowl. Repeat the process two more times. Whisk to mix well and set aside.

In the bowl of a stand mixer fitted with a flat beater, or in a bowl with a hand mixer, beat the egg yolks and lemon zest at high speed until well blended. Gradually add 1 cup of the remaining sugar and beat until the mixture is thick and creamy and forms a wide ribbon when some of the mixture is lifted and dropped back over the remainder, about 5 minutes if using a stand mixer, or about 10 minutes if using a hand mixer. Add 1/4 cup water and the vanilla and lemon extracts and blend well.

Using the stand mixer fitted with a wire whip or hand mixer with clean beaters, in a clean metal bowl, beat the egg whites at low speed until frothy bubbles cover the surface. Add the cream of tartar, increase the speed to medium, and beat until very soft, billowy mounds form when the beater is slowly raised. With the mixer running, gradually add the remaining 1/4 cup sugar, about 1 tablespoon at a time, and beat until the whites form peaks that are stiff but still moist when the beater is raised.

Immediately sift the flour mixture over the egg yolk mixture, then add one-fourth of the egg whites and, using a large balloon whisk or rubber spatula, quickly and gently fold the mixture as directed on page 16 just until the flour mixture and whites disappear. In the same way, gently fold in the remaining whites; avoid overblending, which will deflate the batter.

Scrape the batter into the reserved pan and smooth the surface with a rubber spatula. Bake until the cake is golden and springs back when lightly touched in the center with your fingertip and a wooden skewer inserted into the center of the cake

comes out clean, about 40 minutes; to prevent falling, do not open the oven door until near the end of the minimum baking time.

Remove the pan to a work surface and turn it upside down, resting the rim of the springform pan on 3 or 4 same-sized glasses or the center hole of the tube pan over a long-necked bottle or metal funnel to elevate the pan. Let stand in a draft-free area until the cake is cooled completely, at least $1^1/_2$ hours, then remove the cake from the pan as directed on page 17.

Using a small, sharp knife and your fingertips, scrape and pull off the crust from the top and bottom of the cake.

Use the cake as directed in other recipes, or slice horizontally into 2 or 3 layers as directed on page 18, prepare a favorite filling and/or frosting, and fill and frost the cake as directed on pages 18–19.

Angel Food Cake

This fat-free American hallmark relies on whipped egg whites to achieve billowy heights. Angel food cakes are baked in ungreased pans so that the airy batter can cling to the sides as it rises during baking and the cake will not fall out when hung upside down to cool. ❆ Leave the cake plain for serving with fresh fruit or a favorite dessert sauce. Alternatively drizzle with one of the glazes on pages 104–105; crown with Maple Meringue Frosting (page 115), as shown; or frost with Fluffy White Frosting (page 116), Crème Fraîche Frosting (page 110), or other favorite light frosting. For a fancier presentation, slice the cake into two or three layers, sandwich with Whipped Cream (page 109) and lightly sweetened seasonal berries, and top with more cream. ❆ Forget the old advice about using a special pronged cutter or two forks to separate the cake into pieces. A regular serrated knife works best.

MAKES 12 SERVINGS.

*P*osition racks so that the cake will bake in the middle of an oven and preheat the oven to 325° F. Select a 10-inch angel food or other straight tube pan with a removable bottom; do not grease or line. Set aside.

Place the flour, salt, and ¾ cup of the sugar together in a strainer or sifter and sift into a bowl. Repeat the process two more times. Whisk to mix well and set aside.

In the metal bowl of a stand mixer fitted with a wire whip, or in a metal bowl with a hand mixer, beat the egg whites at low speed until frothy bubbles cover the surface. Add the cream of tartar, increase the speed to medium, and beat until very soft, billowy mounds form when the beater is slowly raised. With the mixer running, gradually add the remaining ¾ cup sugar, about 1 tablespoon at a time, and beat until the whites are shiny and form soft peaks when the beater is raised; avoid overbeating for maximum volume in the cake. Add the vanilla and blend well.

Sift about ¼ cup of the flour mixture over the whites. Using a large balloon whisk or rubber spatula, quickly and gently fold the mixture as directed on page 16 just until the flour mixture is incorporated. In the same way, quickly and gently fold in the remaining flour mixture in ¼-cup increments; the flour mixture must be well incorporated but avoid overmixing and deflating the batter too much.

Gently scrape the batter into the reserved pan and smooth the surface with a rubber spatula. Bake until the cake springs back when lightly touched in the thickest part with your fingertip and a wooden skewer inserted into the thickest part of the

1 cup cake flour

¼ teaspoon salt

1½ cups sugar

2 cups egg whites (from about 16 eggs),
  at room temperature

2 teaspoons cream of tartar

2 teaspoons pure vanilla extract

recipe continues ➤

cake comes out clean, about 50 minutes; to prevent falling, do not open the oven door until near the end of the minimum baking time. (Cracks in the surface are normal.)

Remove the pan to a work surface and turn it upside down, resting the center hole of the pan over a long-necked bottle or metal funnel to elevate the pan. Let stand in a draft-free area until the cake is cooled completely, at least $1\frac{1}{2}$ hours, then remove the cake from the pan as directed on page 17.

Transfer to a serving plate and use a long serrated knife and sawing motions to cut the cake.

Chiffon Cake

After two decades of carefully guarding his secret recipe, making his special cake only for the reigning royalty of the silver screen, the Hollywood baker-inventor Harry Baker sold his formula to General Mills, who gave his innovation the now-famous name chiffon cake. With numerous variations, it became a nationwide sensation during the late 1940s and into the 1950s, and today is still appreciated for its light and springy texture. ❈ Chiffon cakes, like angel food cakes, are baked in ungreased pans so that the batter can cling to the sides as it rises during baking and the cake will not fall out when hung upside down to cool. ❈ For the photograph, I baked the orange variation and adorned it with stars cut out from thinly rolled commercial marzipan and painted with silver decorating paint from a cake-decorating supply store.

MAKES 12 SERVINGS.

$\mathcal{P}$osition racks so that the cake will bake in the middle of an oven and preheat the oven to 325° F. Select a 10-inch angel food or other straight tube pan with a removable bottom; do not grease or line. Set aside.

Place the flour, 1¼ cups of the granulated sugar, the baking powder, and salt together in a strainer or sifter and sift into a bowl. Whisk to mix well. Add ³⁄₄ cup water, the oil, egg yolks, lemon zest, and vanilla. Beat with an electric mixer at medium speed until very smooth, about 1 minute. Set aside.

In the metal bowl of a stand mixer fitted with a wire whip, or in a metal bowl with a hand mixer and clean beaters, beat the egg whites at low speed until frothy bubbles cover the surface. Add the cream of tartar, increase the speed to medium, and beat until very soft, billowy mounds form when the beater is slowly raised. With the mixer running, gradually add the remaining ¼ cup sugar, about 1 tablespoon at a time, and beat until very thick and stiff but not quite dry, about 6 minutes if using a stand mixer, or about 10 minutes if using a hand mixer. (It is important that the whites not be underbeaten; they should be stiffer than for angel food cake or meringue.)

Transfer about one-fourth of the egg whites to the cake batter and stir gently to incorporate and lighten the mixture. Add the remaining egg whites and, using a large balloon whisk or rubber spatula, gently fold them as directed on page 16 into the batter just until incorporated.

Gently scrape the batter into the reserved pan and smooth the surface with a rubber spatula. Bake until the cake springs back when lightly touched in the thickest part with your fingertip and a wooden skewer inserted into the thickest part of the cake

2 cups cake flour

1½ cups granulated sugar

2 teaspoons baking powder

1 teaspoon salt

½ cup canola or other high-quality flavorless vegetable oil

½ cup egg yolks (from 6 or 7 eggs), at room temperature, lightly beaten

2 teaspoons grated or minced fresh lemon zest

1 tablespoon pure vanilla extract

1¼ cups egg whites (from about 10 eggs), at room temperature

1 teaspoon cream of tartar

Powdered sugar for dusting (optional)

recipe continues ➤

Chiffon Cake, orange variation

comes out clean, about 1 hour; to prevent falling, do not open the oven door until near the end of the minimum baking time.

Remove the pan to a work surface and turn it upside down, resting the center hole of the pan over a long-necked bottle or metal funnel to elevate the pan. Let stand in a draft-free area until the cake is cooled completely, at least 1½ hours, then remove the cake from the pan as directed on page 17.

Transfer the cake to a serving plate and dust with powdered sugar (if using). Use a long serrated knife and sawing motions to cut the cake.

Butterscotch Chiffon Cake

Substitute $^3/_4$ cup firmly packed dark brown sugar for $^3/_4$ cup of the granulated sugar. Glaze the cooled cake with Old-fashioned Caramel Frosting (page 118).

Chocolate Chiffon Cake

Substitute $^1/_2$ cup unsweetened cocoa for $^1/_2$ cup of the flour. Omit the lemon zest. Spoon Chocolate Glaze (page 104) over the cooled cake.

Coffee Chiffon Cake

Substitute $^1/_4$ cup coffee-flavored liqueur or 1 tablespoon instant espresso dissolved in $^1/_4$ cup hot water for $^1/_4$ cup of the water. Omit the lemon zest. Use for Coffee Crunch Cake (page 87), or spoon Coffee Glaze (page 105) over the cooled cake.

Guava or Passion Fruit Chiffon Cake

Substitute fresh or thawed frozen guava pulp or passion fruit juice or thawed frozen juice concentrate for the water. If desired, add a touch of pink or red food coloring (for guava) or orange or yellow food coloring (for passion fruit) along with the vanilla to simulate the fresh fruit color. Spoon Guava or Passion Fruit Glaze (page 105) over the cooled cake. Alternatively, slice the cooled cake into 3 layers and fill with Fruit Pudding Filling (page 107) made with guava or passion fruit. Stir $^1/_4$ cup pulp or juice concentrate and a touch of pink or red food coloring (for guava) or orange or yellow food coloring (for passion fruit) into Whipped Cream Frosting (page 109) and frost the top and sides of the cake, then drizzle $^1/_4$ cup of the same pulp or juice concentrate over the top and swirl with a spatula.

Lemon or Lime Chiffon Cake

Substitute 3 tablespoons freshly squeezed lemon or lime juice for 3 tablespoons of the water. Add an additional 1 tablespoon finely grated or minced fresh lemon or lime zest. Reduce the vanilla to 2 teaspoons and add 1 teaspoon pure lemon extract. Spoon Citrus Glaze (page 104) made with lemon or lime juice and zest over the cooled cake.

Orange or Tangerine Chiffon Cake

Substitute freshly squeezed orange or tangerine juice for the water and 3 tablespoons finely grated or minced fresh orange or tangerine zest for the lemon zest. Reduce the vanilla to $2^1/_2$ teaspoons and add $^1/_2$ teaspoon pure orange extract. Spoon Citrus Glaze (page 104) made with orange or tangerine juice and zest over the cooled cake.

Cake Roll

Any sponge cake can be baked as a thin sheet for filling and rolling. Be sure to begin checking for doneness early to prevent overcooking and drying, which makes the cake difficult to roll. ❀ *Spread the cooled cake with about 1½ cups good jelly or jam to create a classic jelly roll and dust the roll with powdered sugar. Or prepare 2 to 3 cups of one of the curds on page 108, Custard Filling (page 106), Whipped Cream (page 109), Ganache (page 117), or another favorite filling and use as directed. For an ice cream cake roll, soften your favorite ice cream to spreading consistency, spread it over the cake, roll it up, wrap tightly in aluminum foil, and freeze until the ice cream is firm.* ❀ *The rolled cake may be frosted with Whipped Cream Frosting (page 109), Cream Cheese Frosting (page 111), Ganache (page 117), Fluffy White Frosting (page 116), or another complementary frosting.*

MAKES 8 SERVINGS.

Batter for Genoise (page 31), Hot-Milk Sponge Cake (page 33), or American Sponge Cake (page 36), or ½ batter for Chiffon Cake (page 41)

Soaking Syrup (page 106; optional)

Filling (see recipe introduction)

Frosting (see recipe introduction; optional)

Powdered sugar for dusting (if not using frosting)

Position racks so that the cake will bake in the lower third of an oven and preheat the oven to 350° F. Grease and line a 17-by-12-inch jelly-roll or half-sheet pan as directed on page 14. Set aside.

Prepare the selected cake batter as directed.

Scrape the batter into the prepared pan and smooth the surface with an offset spatula as evenly as possible, making certain that the edges and corners are as thick as the center. Bake until the cake springs back when lightly touched in the center with your fingertip and a wooden skewer inserted in several places throughout the cake comes out clean, 10 to 20 minutes; check early and frequently to prevent overbrowning and drying.

Remove the pan to a wire rack to cool completely.

Using a small, sharp knife and your fingertips, scrape and pull off the brown crust from the top of the cake. Run a metal spatula or table knife along the two unlined sides to loosen the cake from the pan. Invert the cake onto a large sheet of aluminum foil and peel off the parchment liner.

Prepare the Soaking Syrup (if using genoise), selected filling, and frosting (if using) as directed. Drizzle the cake evenly with syrup (if using) as directed on page 18 and spread the filling evenly over the cake.

Starting at a long edge of the cake, tightly fold and press about 1 inch of the cake over the filling. Using the sheet of foil underneath the cake to lift the cake, continue rolling the cake as compactly as possible. Using a sharp knife, trim off the ragged ends.

Slide a large cake spatula or rimless baking sheet underneath the cake and transfer it, seam side down, to a serving platter.

Spread with frosting (if using). Cover and refrigerate for up to several hours.

If not frosted, dust the roll with powdered sugar just before serving. Slice crosswise to serve.

Crumb-Topped Coffee Cake

When Alma Tudal of Tudal Winery in the Napa Valley shared this family recipe, which the Tudals call Hungarian Coffee Cake, she emphasized that the amount of nutmeg is correctly listed as a full tablespoon, a wonderful amount. My adaptation gives the option of a rich butter taste instead of oil and omits the baking soda originally called for to appreciate more fully the tangy flavor of the buttermilk.❋ This rustic cake with a homey crumb topping is equally delicious for breakfast or a midmorning or afternoon treat.

MAKES 9 SERVINGS.

2½ cups all-purpose flour

1 cup firmly packed light brown sugar

¾ cup granulated sugar

1 tablespoon freshly grated nutmeg

1 teaspoon salt

⅛ teaspoon ground cloves

¾ cup (1½ sticks) unsalted butter, melted and cooled slightly, or canola or other high-quality vegetable oil

2 teaspoons baking powder

1 cup buttermilk, at room temperature

2 eggs, at room temperature, lightly beaten

1 cup chopped walnuts or other nuts

2 tablespoons granulated sugar mixed with 2 teaspoons ground cinnamon for sprinkling

Position racks so that the cake will bake in the middle of an oven and preheat the oven to 350° F. Grease a 9-inch square pan as directed on page 15; do not line or flour it. Set aside.

Place the flour, brown and granulated sugars, nutmeg, salt, and cloves together in a strainer or sifter and sift into a large bowl. Whisk to mix well. Using a spoon, form a well in the middle of the dry ingredients, then pour in the butter or oil and stir, breaking up clumps, until the mixture resembles coarse bread crumbs. Remove ¾ cup of the mixture to a small bowl and reserve for later use.

Stir the baking powder into the mixture in the large bowl. Add the buttermilk and eggs and beat with an electric mixer at medium speed until smooth, about 1 minute.

Scrape the batter into the prepared pan and smooth the surface with a rubber spatula. Evenly distribute the reserved crumb mixture over the top, then scatter the nuts over it and sprinkle with the sugar-cinnamon mixture. Bake until the cake springs back when lightly touched in the center with your fingertip and a wooden skewer inserted into the center of the cake comes out clean, 45 to 50 minutes; if the top begins to brown too quickly during baking, cover loosely with aluminum foil.

Remove the pan to a wire rack to cool for at least 15 minutes. Cut into squares and serve warm or at room temperature directly from the pan.

Three-Milk Cake

Following a holiday in Costa Rica, my friend Peter Olsen introduced me to pastel tres leches, *popular throughout Latin America. Sweetened condensed milk, a key ingredient, was my baby formula, so the dessert was an immediate hit with my palate.* ❋ *Three milks are whisked together and then poured over the warm cake. Amazingly, it absorbs all of the mixture. As the cake sits, however, some of the milk oozes out and forms a delectable sauce. Although I like to turn the cake out of the pan for presentation, it can be frosted in the pan and served directly from it. Use a spoon to ladle some of the sauce onto each plate.*

MAKES 8 SERVINGS.

1 1/4 cups all-purpose flour

1 1/4 teaspoons baking powder

1/4 teaspoon salt

4 eggs, at room temperature, separated
 and yolks lightly beaten

1/2 teaspoon cream of tartar

1 cup sugar

1 tablespoon finely grated or minced
 fresh lime zest

1 teaspoon pure vanilla extract

1/3 cup whole milk, at room temperature

1 can (12 ounces) evaporated milk

1 can (14 ounces) sweetened condensed
 milk

1 cup heavy (whipping) cream

Fluffy White Frosting (page 116)

Position racks so that the cake will bake in the middle of an oven and preheat the oven to 350° F. Grease a 9-inch round cake pan as directed on page 15; do not line or flour it. Set aside.

Place the flour, baking powder, and salt together in a strainer or sifter and sift into a bowl. Repeat the process two more times. Whisk to mix well and set aside.

In the metal bowl of a stand mixer fitted with a wire whip, or in a metal bowl with a hand mixer, beat the egg whites at low speed until frothy bubbles cover the surface. Add the cream of tartar, increase the speed to medium-high, and beat until soft peaks form when the beater is slowly raised. With the mixer running, gradually add the sugar and beat until the whites form peaks that are stiff but still moist when the beater is raised. Slowly drizzle in the egg yolks and beat well; stop at least once to scrape the sides of the bowl. Add the lime zest and vanilla and blend well.

Using the mixer on low speed or a rubber spatula, fold in about one-third of the flour mixture, then half of the whole milk, scraping the sides of the bowl and folding just until the ingredients are incorporated. In the same manner, fold in half of the remaining flour mixture, then the remaining whole milk, and finally the remaining flour mixture.

Scrape the batter into the prepared pan and smooth the surface with a rubber spatula. Bake until the cake springs back when lightly touched in the center with your fingertip and a wooden skewer inserted into the center of the cake comes out clean, about 30 minutes. Remove the pan to a wire rack to cool for 5 to 10 minutes.

recipe continues ➤

Meanwhile, in a measuring cup or pitcher, combine the canned milks and the cream and whisk to blend well.

Prick the top of the cake at 1-inch intervals all over with a wooden skewer. Slowly pour the milk mixture evenly over the cake. Let cool completely, then cover tightly and refrigerate for at least several hours or up to overnight; return to room temperature before frosting.

Prepare the Fluffy White Frosting as directed. Run a small metal spatula or table knife around the edges to loosen the cake from the sides of the pan. Invert a rimmed serving plate that can contain the sauce that may ooze from the cake over the pan, invert the plate and pan together, and lift off the pan. Spread the sides and top of the cake with the frosting, mounding high on the top.

Lemon Cake

Lemon Cake

Tangy and moist, this cake is tantalizing on its own or with fresh summer berries on the side.

MAKES 12 SERVINGS.

Position racks so that the cake will bake in the middle of an oven and preheat the oven to 350° F. Grease and flour a 10-inch Bundt or other fluted tube pan as directed on page 14. Set aside.

Place the flour, baking powder, and salt together in a strainer or sifter and sift into a bowl. Repeat the process two more times. Whisk to mix well and set aside.

In the bowl of a stand mixer fitted with a flat beater, or in a bowl with a hand mixer, beat the butter at medium speed until soft and creamy, about 45 seconds. With the mixer still running, slowly add the sugar, then stop the mixer and scrape the mixture that clings to the sides of the bowl into the center. Add the lemon zest and continue beating at medium speed until the mixture is very light and fluffy, about 5 minutes. Slowly drizzle in the eggs and beat well; stop at least once to scrape the sides of the bowl. Add the lemon and vanilla extracts and blend well.

Using the mixer on low speed or a rubber spatula, fold in about one-third of the flour mixture, then half of the buttermilk and lemon juice, scraping the sides of the bowl and folding just until the ingredients are incorporated. In the same manner, fold in half of the remaining flour mixture, then the remaining buttermilk and lemon juice, and finally the remaining flour mixture.

Scrape the batter into the prepared pan and smooth the surface with a rubber spatula. Bake until the cake springs back when lightly touched in the thickest part with your fingertip and a wooden skewer inserted into the thickest part of the cake comes out clean, about 1 hour.

When the cake is done, remove the pan to a wire rack. Using a wooden skewer, poke the surface of the cake all over with holes about 1-inch deep. Then using a pastry brush, cover with some of the glaze. Let cool for about 5 minutes, then turn the cake out top side up onto the rack as directed on page 17. Pierce the top of the cake all over with holes and brush the top and sides of the cake with several coats of the remaining glaze, using all of the mixture. Set aside to cool completely.

3 cups all-purpose flour

1 tablespoon baking power

3/4 teaspoon salt

1 cup (2 sticks) unsalted butter, at room temperature

2 cups sugar

2 tablespoons finely grated or minced fresh lemon zest

4 eggs, at room temperature, lightly beaten

1 tablespoon pure lemon extract

1 teaspoon pure vanilla extract

1 cup buttermilk, at room temperature

1/4 cup freshly squeezed lemon juice

Citrus Glaze (page 104) made with lemon juice and zest

Upside-Down Tropical Fruit Cake

Rosa Smith, our housekeeper back in Jonesville, Louisiana, often begged my mother to make her a classic pineapple upside-down cake studded with cherries and baked in a cast-iron skillet. Although canned pineapple still makes a great cake, I'm crazy about my updated version made with fresh tropical fruit, especially mango, which I've shown in the photograph. I also bake the cake in a regular cake pan for easier removal.❋ For a nontropical version, substitute apple, nectarine, peach, pear, or plum slices or whole blackberries, blueberries, or raspberries for the tropical fruits.

MAKES 8 SERVINGS.

$^3/_4$ cup (1$^1/_2$ sticks) unsalted butter, at room temperature

$^3/_4$ cup firmly packed light brown sugar

2$^1/_2$ cups sliced banana, mango, papaya, or pineapple

1$^1/_2$ cups all-purpose flour

1$^1/_2$ teaspoons baking powder

$^1/_2$ teaspoon salt

$^3/_4$ cup granulated sugar

2 eggs, at room temperature, lightly beaten

1 teaspoon pure vanilla extract

$^1/_2$ cup whole milk, at room temperature

Position racks so that the cake will bake in the middle of an oven and preheat the oven to 350° F. Grease a 9-inch round cake pan as directed on page 15; do not line or flour it. Set aside.

In a saucepan, combine $^1/_4$ cup of the butter and the brown sugar. Place over medium heat and cook, stirring occasionally, until the butter melts and the mixture is slightly caramelized, about 3 minutes. Pour into the prepared cake pan and quickly swirl to coat evenly.

Arrange the fruit slices in slightly overlapping concentric circles over the melted sugar mixture. Set aside.

Place the flour, baking powder, and salt together in a strainer or sifter and sift into a bowl. Repeat the process two more times. Whisk to mix well and set aside.

In the bowl of a stand mixer fitted with a flat beater, or in a bowl with a hand mixer, beat the remaining $^1/_2$ cup butter at medium speed until soft and creamy, about 45 seconds. With the mixer still running, slowly add the granulated sugar, then stop the mixer and scrape the mixture that clings to the sides of the bowl into the center. Continue beating at medium speed until the mixture is very light and fluffy, about 5 minutes. Slowly drizzle in the eggs and beat well; stop at least once to scrape the sides of the bowl. Add the vanilla and blend well.

Using the mixer on low speed or a rubber spatula, fold in about one-third of the flour mixture, then half of the milk, scraping the sides of the bowl and folding just until the ingredients are incorporated. In the same manner, fold in half of the remaining flour mixture, then the remaining milk, and finally, the remaining flour mixture.

Scrape the batter over the fruit in the pan and smooth the surface with a rubber spatula. Bake until the cake springs back when lightly touched in the center with your

fingertip and a wooden skewer inserted into the center of the cake comes out clean, 50 to 55 minutes.

Remove the pan to a work surface and let stand for about 2 minutes.

Run a metal spatula or table knife around the inside edge of the pan to loosen the cake from the sides of the pan. Invert a serving plate over the pan, invert the plate and pan together, and lift off the pan. If any fruit sticks to the pan, remove it with a spatula and reposition it on the cake. Set aside to cool slightly before serving warm or at room temperature.

Plantation Cake

Ed Broussard, my late friend from Baptist seminary days in New Orleans, often baked a "fruit cocktail cake" to end his wonderful Cajun feasts. It was made with canned fruit cocktail and pecan topping and was the inspiration for this gooey confection. ❁ *I've given the venerable favorite a tropical treatment by combining the best of plantation crops: pineapple, macadamia nuts, vanilla, sugar, and coconut. Pineapple chunks as packed seem a bit too large and crushed pineapple too indistinctive in this cake, so I take the time to cut the chunks into smaller pieces.*

MAKES 12 SERVINGS.

1 cup coarsely chopped macadamia nuts

$^1/_2$ cup firmly packed light brown sugar

$^1/_4$ cup ($^1/_2$ stick) unsalted butter, at room
temperature

1 can (20 ounces) pineapple chunks
packed in juice

3 cups all-purpose flour

1$^1/_2$ cups granulated sugar

1 tablespoon baking powder

1 teaspoon salt

3 eggs, at room temperature, lightly beaten

2 teaspoons pure vanilla extract

1 cup Grated or Shredded Fresh Coconut
(page 124) or packaged sweetened
coconut

1 can (14 ounces) sweetened condensed
milk (not evaporated milk)

*P*osition racks so that the cake will bake in the middle of an oven and preheat the oven to 350° F. Grease a 13-by-9-inch pan as directed on page 15; do not line or flour it. Set aside.

In a bowl, combine the nuts, brown sugar, and butter. Using your fingertips, blend well. Set aside.

Drain the pineapple chunks through a strainer set over a bowl; reserve the juice. Cut each chunk into 4 equal pieces, add to the juice, and set aside.

Place the flour, granulated sugar, baking powder, and salt together in a strainer or sifter and sift into a bowl. Repeat the process two more times. Whisk to mix well. Add the pineapple and juice, eggs, and vanilla and stir until well blended.

Scrape the batter into the prepared pan and smooth the surface with a rubber spatula. Sprinkle the nut mixture evenly over the top. Bake until the cake springs back when lightly touched in the center with your fingertip and a wooden skewer inserted into the center of the cake comes out clean, about 45 minutes.

Meanwhile, in a skillet, place the coconut over medium heat and toast, shaking the pan or stirring frequently, until lightly browned; do not allow to burn. Pour onto a plate to cool.

Just before the cake is done, in a small saucepan or microwave-safe pitcher, heat the condensed milk over medium heat or at full power until warm and pourable.

When the cake is done, remove the pan to a wire rack. Drizzle the condensed milk over the warm cake, sprinkle with the coconut, and set aside to cool completely.

Cut into squares and serve directly from the pan.

Honey Yogurt Cake

I first encountered this tangy cake at an Armenian bakery when I lived in New York. When I moved to San Francisco, I was overjoyed to find a tiny Greek take-out shop that made this specialty. It is common throughout the eastern Mediterranean and individual pieces are usually topped with a nut. ❁ *Yogurt made from goat's milk is particularly good in this cake. You may also choose to add a traditional splash of rose water (available in Middle Eastern and Indian markets) to the cooled syrup.*

MAKES 12 SERVINGS.

HONEY-LEMON SYRUP

1 cup honey

2 tablespoons shredded fresh lemon zest

1/4 cup freshly squeezed lemon juice

2 1/2 cups all-purpose flour

1/2 teaspoon baking powder

1/2 teaspoon baking soda

1/2 teaspoon salt

1/2 cup (1 stick) unsalted butter, at room temperature

2 cups sugar

2 tablespoons grated or minced fresh lemon zest

3 eggs, at room temperature, lightly beaten

1 teaspoon pure lemon extract

1 1/2 cups plain yogurt (not fat free), at room temperature

12 blanched whole almonds or 36 pine nuts, or more if serving smaller pieces

To make the Honey-Lemon Syrup, in a heavy 2-quart saucepan, combine the honey and 1 cup water. Place over medium-high heat and bring to a boil. Reduce the heat to achieve a simmer, stir in the shredded lemon zest, and cook, stirring occasionally, until the consistency of a light syrup, about 20 minutes. Stir in the lemon juice and set aside to cool to room temperature.

Position racks so that the cake will bake in the middle of an oven and preheat the oven to 350° F. Grease a 13-by-9-inch pan as directed on page 15; do not line or flour it. Set aside.

Place the flour, baking powder, baking soda, and salt together in a strainer or sifter and sift into a bowl. Whisk to mix well and set aside.

In the bowl of a stand mixer fitted with a flat beater, or in a bowl with a hand mixer, beat the butter at medium speed until soft and creamy, about 45 seconds. With the mixer still running, slowly add the sugar, then stop the mixer and scrape the mixture that clings to the sides of the bowl into the center. Add the grated or minced lemon zest and continue beating at medium speed until the mixture is very light and fluffy, about 5 minutes. Slowly drizzle in the eggs and beat well; stop at least once to scrape the sides of the bowl. Add the lemon extract and blend well.

Using the mixer on low speed or a rubber spatula, fold in about one-third of the flour mixture, then half of the yogurt, scraping the sides of the bowl and folding just until the ingredients are incorporated. In the same manner, fold in half of the remaining flour mixture, then the remaining yogurt, and finally the remaining flour mixture.

Scrape the batter into the prepared pan and smooth the surface with a rubber spatula. Bake until the cake springs back when lightly touched in the center with your fingertip and a wooden skewer inserted into the center of the cake comes out clean, 35 to 40 minutes.

Meanwhile, in a small skillet, place the almonds or pine nuts over medium heat and toast, shaking the pan or stirring frequently, until lightly golden and fragrant, about 5 minutes. Pour onto a plate to cool.

When the cake is done, remove the pan to a wire rack. Using a sharp knife, score the top of the cake to divide it into 12 equal sections, then pierce at 1-inch intervals all over with a wooden skewer. Strain the cooled syrup into a small pitcher, reserving the glazed zest, and pour the syrup evenly over the top of the cake. Arrange 1 almond or 3 pine nuts in the center of each section and sprinkle with the reserved lemon zest. Set aside to cool completely.

Cut along the scored lines and serve directly from the pan.

Very Berry Cake

When fresh berries are not in season, such as around Valentine's Day when a heart-shaped version of this cake seems most appropriate, frozen berries will work well. You'll need about 5 ounces for the cake and an equal amount for the frosting. During berry season, lightly sweeten fresh berries with sugar and let stand to bring out the juices before using; start with about 2 cups for use in both the cake and frosting.

MAKES 12 SERVINGS.

*P*osition racks so that the cake layers will bake in the middle of an oven and preheat the oven to 350° F. Grease and line two 10-inch heart-shaped cake pans or two 9-inch round cake pans as directed on page 14. Set aside.

In a bowl or glass measuring cup, combine the egg whites, milk, and vanilla and whisk to blend well. Set aside.

In the bowl of a stand mixer fitted with a flat beater, or in a bowl with a hand mixer, combine the flour, sugar, baking powder, salt, and Jell-O® and mix at low speed until well blended, about 30 seconds. Add the butter and beat at medium speed until the mixture resembles coarse bread crumbs, about 45 seconds.

Add about 1 cup of the egg white mixture and beat at medium speed if using a stand mixer or high speed if using a hand mixer for 1½ minutes, then stop the mixer and scrape the mixture that clings to the sides of the bowl into the center. Add the remaining egg white mixture and beat at the same speed for 30 seconds, then stop and scrape down the sides of the bowl and beat again until creamy smooth, about 30 seconds. Add the mashed berries and blend well.

Divide the batter evenly between the prepared pans and smooth the surfaces with a rubber spatula. Bake until each cake layer springs back when lightly touched in the center with your fingertip and a wooden skewer inserted into the center of each layer comes out clean, about 30 minutes.

Remove the pans to a wire rack to cool for 5 to 10 minutes, then turn the layers out onto the rack to cool completely as directed on page 17.

Prepare the selected frosting as directed. Fill and frost the cake as directed on pages 18–19. Just before serving, garnish with fresh berries and flowers.

¾ cup egg whites (from about 6 eggs), at room temperature

½ cup whole milk, at room temperature

2 teaspoons pure vanilla extract

2½ cups cake flour

1¾ cups sugar

2½ teaspoons baking powder

¾ teaspoon salt

1 small package (3 ounces) raspberry- or strawberry-flavored Jell-O® or similar gelatin dessert product

¾ cup (1½ sticks) unsalted butter, at room temperature

½ cup mashed drained fresh or thawed frozen raspberries or strawberries, or a combination, at room temperature

Berry Frosting (page 114) or Berry Buttercream (page 112), made with same type berries used in cake

Fresh whole raspberries and/or strawberries for garnish

Pesticide-free miniature roses or rose petals and forget-me-nots for garnish

Meringue Cake

This unique composition of layers of meringue-topped cake sandwiching cream and fresh fruit or jam was passed down from my partner Andrew's grandmother. Grandma Bo called it Blitzkuchen *or* Blitztorte. *An early edition of* The Joy of Cooking *identified* Blitztorte *as a custard-filled predecessor of the whipped-cream-and-fruit-filled version that the authors called a "cream meringue tart."* ❋ *Instead of cream and fruit, I sometimes fill the cake with Custard Filling (page 106), one of the curds on page 108, or traditional Key lime pie filling. Use the basic idea to create your own family favorites.*

MAKES 12 SERVINGS.

$\mathcal{P}$osition racks so that the cake layers will bake in the middle of an oven and preheat the oven to 325° F. Grease two 9-inch round cake pans and line the bottoms as directed on page 14. Set aside.

Place the flour, baking powder, and salt together in a strainer or sifter and sift into a bowl. Repeat the process two more times. Whisk to mix well and set aside.

In the bowl of a stand mixer fitted with a flat beater, or in a bowl with a hand mixer, beat the butter at medium speed until soft and creamy, about 45 seconds. With the mixer still running, slowly add ½ cup of the sugar, then stop the mixer and scrape the mixture that clings to the sides of the bowl into the center. Continue beating at medium speed until the mixture is very light and fluffy, about 5 minutes. Slowly drizzle the egg yolks into the mixture and beat well; stop at least once to scrape the sides of the bowl. Add 1 teaspoon of the vanilla and blend well.

Using the mixer on low speed or a rubber spatula, fold in half of the flour mixture, then the milk, scraping the sides of the bowl and folding just until the ingredients are incorporated. In the same manner, fold in the remaining flour mixture.

Divide the batter evenly between the prepared pans and smooth the surfaces with a rubber spatula; set aside.

Using the stand mixer fitted with a wire whip or hand mixer with clean beaters, in a clean metal bowl, beat the egg whites at medium speed until soft peaks form when the beater is slowly raised. Increase the mixer speed to high and slowly sprinkle in the remaining 1 cup sugar, 1 tablespoon at a time, then add the remaining 1 teaspoon vanilla and beat until the whites form peaks that are very stiff and glossy when the beater is raised.

1 cup all-purpose flour

1 teaspoon baking powder

¼ teaspoon salt

½ cup (1 stick) unsalted butter, at room temperature

1½ cups sugar

4 eggs, at room temperature, separated and yolks lightly beaten

2 teaspoons pure vanilla extract

⅓ cup whole milk, at room temperature

½ cup sliced almonds

Whipped Cream (page 109)

4 cups seasonal berries or peeled and sliced soft fruit such as bananas, mangoes, nectarines, or peaches

Sugar for sweetening berries (optional)

Whole berries with their leaves and blossoms for garnish (optional)

recipe continues ➤

Spread the meringue evenly over the batter in the pans, then scatter the almonds all over the meringue-topped layers. Bake until the meringue is firm and golden brown, about 45 minutes; the surfaces will be irregular and cracked.

Remove the pans to a wire rack to cool completely.

Shortly before serving, prepare the Whipped Cream as directed. If using berries, sweeten with sugar to taste.

To assemble, run a small metal spatula or table knife around the edges to loosen the cake layers from the sides of the pans. Invert a serving plate over one pan, invert the plate and pan together, and lift off the pan, leaving the meringue side down on the plate. Arrange half of the berries or sliced fruit evenly over the cake and cover with half of the whipped cream. Turn out the remaining layer as directed on page 17 and place it, meringue side up, on top of the cream. Garnish with whole berries, leaves, and blossoms (if using). Serve with the remaining cream and berries.

Fresh Ginger Cake

Fresh Ginger Cake

Andrew and I created this cake for an old-style Hawaiian luau to celebrate a special birthday for Auntie Naila. We also enjoy baking this cake in a tube pan and finishing it with Citrus Glaze (page 104) made with lime juice and zest.

MAKES 12 SERVINGS.

Position racks so that the cake layers will bake in the middle of an oven and preheat the oven to 350° F. Grease and line two 9-inch round cake pans as directed on page 14. Set aside.

Place the flour, baking powder, and salt together in a strainer or sifter and sift into a bowl. Repeat the process two more times. Whisk to mix well and set aside.

In the bowl of a stand mixer fitted with a flat beater, or in a bowl with a hand mixer, beat the butter at medium speed until soft and creamy, about 45 seconds. With the mixer still running, slowly add the sugar, then stop the mixer and scrape the mixture that clings to the sides of the bowl into the center. Add the lime zest and continue beating at medium speed until the mixture is very light and fluffy, about 5 minutes. Slowly drizzle in the eggs and beat well; stop at least once to scrape the sides of the bowl. Add the ginger and blend well.

Using the mixer on low speed or a rubber spatula, fold in about one-third of the flour mixture, then half of the milk, scraping the sides of the bowl and folding just until the ingredients are incorporated. In the same manner, fold in half of the remaining flour mixture, then the remaining milk, and finally the remaining flour mixture.

Divide the batter evenly between the prepared pans and smooth the surfaces with a rubber spatula. Bake until each cake layer springs back when lightly touched in the center with your fingertip and a wooden skewer inserted into the center of each layer comes out clean, about 35 minutes.

Remove the pans to a wire rack to cool for 5 to 10 minutes, then turn the layers out onto the rack to cool completely as directed on page 17.

Prepare the Cream Cheese Frosting as directed. Fill and frost the cake as directed on pages 18–19. Place the macadamia nut in the center of the cake, arrange ginger slices to resemble a sunburst or flower around the nut, and sprinkle with lime zest.

3 cups all-purpose flour

1 tablespoon baking powder

1 teaspoon salt

1 cup (2 sticks) unsalted butter, at room temperature

2 cups sugar

2 tablespoons grated or minced fresh lime zest

4 eggs, at room temperature, lightly beaten

1 cup finely grated fresh ginger

1 cup whole milk, at room temperature

Cream Cheese Frosting (page 111), made with macadamia nuts

Whole macadamia nut for garnish

Crystallized ginger slices for garnish

Shredded fresh lime zest for garnish

Southern Coconut Cake

As a young child, I dubbed Mamaw Olivia Belle Keith's coconut cake "live" because that's how the hairy brown coconuts looked to me before she cracked them open. To this day, this old southern delicacy bears the name Live Coconut Cake in my family. Although not as fresh tasting, packaged sweetened coconut also makes a very fine cake; substitute about 4 cups for the fresh coconut. ❆ For a delicious alternative, spread Custard Filling (page 106) or any of the curds on page 108 between the layers, and cover the top and sides with the suggested frosting or with either Ganache (page 117) made with white chocolate or Crème Fraîche Frosting (page 110) before sprinkling with the coconut. I've added a couple of variations on the theme that I also enjoy. Toasted coconut adds a new dimension to the traditional cake, while the chocolate-frosted version is reminiscent of one of my favorite candy bars.

MAKES 12 SERVINGS.

Yellow Cake (page 26)

Grated or Shredded Fresh Coconut (page 124; reserve juice from drained coconut)

Soaking Syrup (page 106), adding reserved coconut juice

Fluffy White Frosting (page 116)

Make and cool the Yellow Cake as directed.

Prepare the Grated or Shredded Fresh Coconut, Soaking Syrup, and Fluffy White Frosting. As directed on pages 18–19, slice each cake layer horizontally in half to create 4 layers total, drizzle evenly with syrup, then fill and frost the cake, sprinkling the coconut over the frosting between the layers and all over the finished cake.

VARIATIONS

Mound of Coconut Cake

Substitute White Cake (page 28) for the Yellow Cake. Prepare a double recipe of Custard Filling (page 106), stir in 2 cups Grated or Shredded Fresh Coconut (page 124) or packaged sweetened coconut, and use to fill the layers as directed on page 18. Frost the top and sides of the cake with Ganache (page 117) made with semisweet chocolate.

Toasted Coconut Cake

Working in batches, place the Grated or Shredded Fresh Coconut in a large skillet and place over medium heat, stirring frequently, until the coconut is toasted to a golden hue; watch carefully to avoid burning. Pour into a bowl to cool. Use as directed in the recipe.

Hawaiian Coconut Cake

In Hawaii, a luau often ends with haupia, *a gelatinous dessert made with coconut milk. This cake has the clean, fresh taste of pure coconut, especially when the filling is made with homemade or thawed frozen high-quality coconut milk (sometimes available labeled "Hawaiian style" in Asian markets) and the cake is finished with fresh rather than packaged coconut.* ❉ *When the large Hawaiian branch of our family gets together, a big cake as shown here is required. I prepare 2 batches of White Cake batter and bake each in a 13-by-9-inch pan, then slice the cakes to create a total of 4 layers and finish with double recipes of the filling and frosting.*

MAKES 12 SERVINGS.

M̶ake and cool the White Cake as directed.

Using a sharp knife, carefully trim off all of the browned crust from the top, bottom, and sides of the cake layers to create completely white layers. Slice each layer horizontally in half to create 4 layers total as directed on page 18.

To make the *Haupia* Filling, in a heavy saucepan, combine the sugar and cornstarch. Gradually whisk in $1\frac{1}{2}$ cups water until the mixture is smooth, then stir in the coconut milk. Place over medium heat and cook, stirring almost constantly, until thickened, about 10 minutes. Remove from the heat and set aside to cool for about 10 minutes.

Fill the cake layers as directed on page 18, spreading about one-fourth of the filling between each layer and on top of the cake. Set aside at room temperature for the filling to set while preparing the frosting.

Prepare the Whipped Cream Frosting as directed. Frost the sides of the cake as directed on page 19, and make a 1-inch border around the outside perimeter of the top of the cake with the frosting, leaving the *haupia* on the top exposed. Generously sprinkle the frosted area with the Grated or Shredded Fresh Coconut or packaged coconut and garnish with orchids (if using).

White Cake (page 28)

HAUPIA FILLING
$\frac{3}{4}$ cup sugar
$\frac{1}{2}$ cup cornstarch
3 cups Fresh Coconut Milk (page 124) or high-quality commercial coconut milk (see recipe introduction)

Whipped Cream Frosting (page 109)
2 cups Grated or Shredded Fresh Coconut (page 124) or packaged sweetened coconut
Pesticide-free, nontoxic small orchids for garnish (optional)

Passion Fruit Cake

The seductive perfumed fragrance and flavor of passion fruit make eating it one of life's greatest pleasures. One bite of this heady concoction transports me to an island paradise. When I can't find a plentiful supply of wrinkled fresh passion fruits in the produce market, I purchase packages of the frozen juice from Latin American markets in San Francisco or use frozen concentrate from Hawaii, where the fruits are known by their ancient Hawaiian name, lilikoi. ❈ *You will need two Genoise or Hot-Milk Sponge Cakes to complete this recipe; due to the delicate structure of these batters, I do not recommend doubling the recipes, but advocate mixing and baking the two cakes separately. If you wish to work ahead, the cooled cakes can be tightly wrapped in plastic wrap and refrigerated for up to 2 days before assembling the cake.*

MAKES 12 SERVINGS.

*Double recipe Passion Fruit Curd
(page 108)*

*2 Genoise (page 31) or Hot-Milk Sponge
Cakes (page 33)*

*Soaking Syrup (page 106), adding
passion fruit liqueur or juice*

*Creamy Curd Frosting (page 108), made
with Passion Fruit Curd*

*Pesticide-free passionflowers for garnish
(optional)*

Prepare the Passion Fruit Curd as directed.

Make and cool 2 of either of the cakes as directed (see recipe introduction).

Prepare the Soaking Syrup as directed. Slice each cake horizontally in half to create 4 layers total and drizzle evenly with syrup as directed on page 18. Fill the layers with Passion Fruit Curd as directed on page 18, spreading about ¾ cup curd between each layer; reserve the remaining curd for the frosting and decorating. Refrigerate for at least 1 hour or up to overnight.

Prepare the Creamy Curd Frosting as directed and frost the top and sides of the cake as directed on page 19.

Spoon about ¼ cup curd onto the center of the cake and pull a spatula through it to create a simple pattern on top of the cake. Garnish with passionflowers (if using).

Bananas Foster Cake

One of my favorite New Orleans desserts is bananas Foster, in which the sliced fruit is quickly cooked in a cinnamon-laced brown sugar syrup,
then flambéed with rum before being scooped over vanilla ice cream. All of those familiar flavors are captured in this cake.

MAKES 12 SERVINGS.

Praline (page 125; optional)

3 cups all-purpose flour

1 tablespoon baking powder

1 teaspoon salt

1 1/2 cups pureed very ripe bananas (from 3
   or 4 bananas)

1/2 cup buttermilk, at room temperature

1 1/4 cups (2 1/2 sticks) unsalted butter, at
   room temperature

2 cups sugar

4 eggs, at room temperature, lightly beaten

2 teaspoons pure vanilla extract

1/4 cup dark brown sugar

2 teaspoons ground cinnamon

4 cups sliced ripe yet firm bananas

2 tablespoons banana liqueur

2 tablespoons dark or light rum

1 1/2 cups Crème Fraîche (page 110) or
   commercial crème fraîche

1 tablespoon powdered sugar, or to taste

1/2 recipe Butterscotch Frosting (page 119)

If using Praline, make as directed and set aside; do not grind until just before using.

Position racks so that the cake layers will bake in the middle of an oven and pre-heat the oven to 350° F. Grease and line two 9-inch round cake pans as directed on page 14. Set aside.

Place the flour, baking powder, and salt together in a strainer or sifter and sift into a bowl. Repeat the process two more times. Whisk to mix well and set aside.

In a bowl or measuring cup, combine the pureed bananas and the buttermilk and blend well. Set aside.

In the bowl of a stand mixer fitted with a flat beater, or in a bowl with a hand mixer, beat 1 cup (2 sticks) of the butter at medium speed until soft and creamy, about 45 seconds. With the mixer still running, slowly add the sugar, then stop the mixer and scrape the mixture that clings to the sides of the bowl into the center. Continue beating at medium speed until the mixture is very light and fluffy, about 5 minutes. Slowly drizzle in the eggs and beat well; stop at least once to scrape the sides of the bowl. Add the vanilla and blend well.

Using the mixer on low speed or a rubber spatula, fold in about one-third of the flour mixture, then half of the banana mixture, scraping the sides of the bowl and folding just until the ingredients are incorporated. In the same manner, fold in half of the remaining flour mixture, then the remaining banana mixture, and finally the re-maining flour mixture.

Divide the batter evenly between the prepared pans and smooth the surfaces with a rubber spatula. Bake until each cake layer springs back when touched in the center with your fingertip and a wooden skewer inserted into the center of each layer comes out clean, about 30 minutes.

Remove the pans to a wire rack to cool for 5 to 10 minutes, then turn the layers out onto the rack to cool completely as directed on page 17.

In a skillet, melt the remaining $\frac{1}{4}$ cup ($\frac{1}{2}$ stick) butter over medium-high heat. Add the brown sugar and cinnamon and stir until the sugar melts, about 2 minutes. Add the sliced bananas and cook, stirring frequently, until the slices are soft but still hold their shape, 2 to 3 minutes. Stir in the banana liqueur and rum and cook for about 30 seconds longer. Transfer to a plate to cool completely.

Whip the crème fraîche and powdered sugar as directed for Whipped Cream on page 109. Set aside.

Center a cake layer on a serving plate. Arrange half of the cooked banana slices over the cake in a single layer. Spoon half of the whipped crème fraîche onto the layer of slices and smooth to cover and fill holes between the slices. Cover with the other cake layer and spread the remaining whipped crème fraîche evenly over the top. Arrange the remaining banana slices over the top in a single layer.

Prepare the Butterscotch Frosting as directed. Frost the sides of the cake as directed on page 19. If desired, pipe a border of frosting around the perimeter of the top of the cake. Finely grind some of the praline (if using) and sprinkle over the border of frosting or the banana slices.

Gingered Carrot Cake

Many carrot cake recipes end up tasting like spice cakes with only a hint of carrot flavor. My version lets the carrots shine through, complemented by the addition of ginger and apricot and a zesty orange frosting. Sugaring and draining the carrots means a large amount can be used in the batter, which results in a more intense carrot color and flavor in the finished cake, a wonderful technique suggested by Marie Piraino and Jamie Morris.

MAKES 12 SERVINGS.

Place the carrots in a colander set over a bowl. Sprinkle with ³⁄₄ cup of the sugar and set aside to drain, stirring occasionally, for about 25 minutes.

Position racks so that the cake layers will bake in the middle of an oven and preheat the oven to 350° F. Grease and line two 9-inch round cake pans as directed on page 14. Set aside.

Place the flour, baking powder, baking soda, and salt together in a strainer or sifter and sift into a bowl. Repeat the process two more times. Whisk to mix well and set aside.

In the bowl of a stand mixer fitted with a flat beater, or in a bowl with a hand mixer, beat the melted butter and the remaining 2 cups sugar until well blended. Slowly drizzle in the eggs and beat well; stop at least once to scrape the mixture that clings to the sides of the bowl into the center.

Gently squeeze the carrots to release as much moisture as possible and add to the butter mixture; discard the liquid drained from the carrots. Add the preserved or crystallized ginger, apricots, and fresh ginger and mix at low speed until well blended.

Using the mixer on low speed or a rubber spatula, fold in the flour mixture just until incorporated.

Divide the batter evenly between the prepared pans and smooth the surfaces with a rubber spatula. Bake until each cake layer springs back when lightly touched in the center with your fingertip and a wooden skewer inserted into the center of each layer comes out clean, about 40 minutes.

Transfer the pans to a wire rack to cool for about 10 minutes, then turn the layers out onto the rack to cool completely as directed on page 17.

Prepare the Orange Cream Cheese Frosting as directed. Fill and frost the cake as directed on pages 18–19.

6 cups finely chopped or shredded carrots (about 2 pounds)

2³⁄₄ cups sugar

2¹⁄₂ cups all-purpose flour

2 teaspoons baking powder

¹⁄₂ teaspoon baking soda

³⁄₄ teaspoon salt

³⁄₄ cup (1¹⁄₂ sticks) unsalted butter, melted and cooled slightly

4 eggs, at room temperature, lightly beaten

¹⁄₂ cup finely chopped drained preserved ginger in syrup (available in Asian markets and specialty foods stores) or crystallized ginger

¹⁄₄ cup finely chopped dried apricots

1 tablespoon grated or minced fresh ginger

Orange Cream Cheese Frosting (page 111)

Heirloom Apple Cake

Although this moist cake is wonderful served warm from the oven with vanilla ice cream or whipped cream, it is even more delectable when glazed, as shown, with Old-fashioned Caramel Frosting (page 118) to resemble a big caramel apple. Or cover with Butterscotch Frosting (page 119) or Cream Cheese Frosting (page 111). ❈ *Choose good baking apples, preferably fresh from your backyard, a roadside stand, or a farmers' market. Look for Baldwin, Cortland, Golden Delicious, Gravenstein, Ida Red, Northern Spy, or local heirloom varieties with plenty of flavor and juicy texture. Tart apples such as Granny Smith are best left for pies or crisps.*

MAKES 12 SERVINGS.

*P*osition racks so that the cake will bake in the middle of an oven and preheat the oven to 350° F. Grease and flour a 10-inch Bundt or other fluted tube pan as directed on page 14. Set aside.

Toast the nuts as directed on page 123, then chop and set aside.

Place the flour, baking powder, and salt together in a strainer or sifter and sift into a bowl. Whisk to mix well and set aside.

In the bowl of a stand mixer fitted with a flat beater, or in a bowl with a hand mixer, combine the sugar, oil, eggs, and vanilla and beat at medium speed until smooth, about 1 minute.

Using the mixer on low speed, fold in the flour mixture just until incorporated, then fold in the apples, raisins, and nuts until well blended.

Scrape the stiff batter into the prepared pan and smooth the surface with a rubber spatula. Bake until the cake springs back when lightly touched in the thickest part with your fingertip and a wooden skewer inserted into the thickest part of the cake comes out clean, 1 hour to $1\frac{1}{4}$ hours.

Remove the pan to a wire rack to cool for about 15 minutes, then turn the cake out onto the rack to cool completely as directed on page 17.

1 cup pecans or walnuts

$2\frac{1}{2}$ cups all-purpose flour

$2\frac{1}{2}$ teaspoons baking powder

1 teaspoon salt

2 cups sugar

$1\frac{1}{2}$ cups canola or other high-quality flavorless vegetable oil

2 eggs, at room temperature

2 teaspoons pure vanilla extract

3 cups peeled, cored, and finely chopped flavorful baking apples (see recipe introduction)

1 cup raisins

Devil's Food Cake

I enjoy finishing this great American standard with rich ganache. When I'm feeling extravagant, I make a double batch of the creamier truffle variation of ganache, then slice each cake layer horizontally in half to create 4 layers total and lavishly spread the ganache to make a chocolate truffle cake, shown here. ❋ *Other finishing options include Fluffy White Frosting (page 116) drizzled with melted semisweet chocolate, Chocolate Cream Cheese Frosting (page 111), Peanut Butter Frosting (page 115), Chocolate Frosting (page 114), Old-fashioned Caramel Frosting (page 118), Butterscotch Frosting (page 119), or Whipped Cream Frosting (page 109) piled high with shavings or curls of semisweet chocolate.*

MAKES 12 SERVINGS.

$^3/_4$ cup unsweetened natural cocoa (not
    Dutch-processed)
1$^1/_2$ cups boiling water or hot strong
    brewed coffee
$^3/_4$ cup whole milk
3 cups all-purpose flour
1 teaspoon baking soda
$^3/_4$ teaspoon salt
$^3/_4$ cup (1$^1/_2$ sticks) unsalted butter, at
    room temperature
2$^1/_4$ cups sugar
3 eggs, at room temperature, lightly beaten
1$^1/_2$ teaspoons pure vanilla extract
Ganache (page 117)
Seedless raspberry jam (a favorite recipe or
    high-quality commercial product) for
    spreading (optional)

*P*osition racks so that the cake layers will bake in the middle of an oven and preheat the oven to 350° F. Grease and line two 9-inch round cake pans as directed on page 14. Set aside.

Place the cocoa in a heatproof bowl or glass measuring cup, slowly add the boiling water or hot coffee, and stir until smooth. Stir in the milk and set aside to cool to room temperature.

Place the flour, baking soda, and salt together in a strainer or sifter and sift into a bowl. Repeat the process two more times. Whisk to mix well and set aside.

In the bowl of a stand mixer fitted with a flat beater, or in a bowl with a hand mixer, beat the butter at medium speed until soft and creamy, about 45 seconds. With the mixer still running, slowly add the sugar, then stop the mixer and scrape the mixture that clings to the sides of the bowl into the center. Continue beating at medium speed until the mixture is very light and fluffy, about 5 minutes. Slowly drizzle in the eggs and beat well; stop at least once to scrape the sides of the bowl. Add the vanilla and blend well.

Using the mixer on low speed or a rubber spatula, fold in about one-third of the flour mixture, then half of the cocoa mixture, scraping the sides of the bowl and folding just until the ingredients are incorporated. In the same manner, fold in half of the remaining flour mixture, then the remaining cocoa mixture, and finally the remaining flour mixture.

Divide the batter evenly between the prepared pans and smooth the tops with a rubber spatula. Bake until each cake layer springs back when lightly touched in the

center with your fingertip and a wooden skewer inserted into the center of each layer comes out clean, about 35 minutes.

Remove the pans to a wire rack to cool for 5 to 10 minutes, then turn the layers out onto the rack to cool completely as directed on page 17.

Prepare the Ganache as directed.

Fill and frost the cake with the Ganache as directed on pages 18–19, spreading each layer with a thin layer of jam (if using) before spreading with the Ganache.

Grand Turtle Cake

My mother introduced me to this delectable creation inspired by the original Neiman-Marcus chocolate-caramel-pecan candies sold as turtles. Since my nephew Devereux has always called his grandmother Grand Turtle, I've dubbed her cake idea Grand Turtle Cake. By any name it is a grand and gooey sensation that is easy to prepare and disappears quickly. ❊ *Mother uses a devil's food cake mix for her batter. I prefer to stir up the batter for the traditional nondairy and eggless cake known as crazy chocolate cake, a favorite from my partner Andrew's childhood, that is as quick and easy as a mix.* ❊ *Serve with dollops of lightly sweetened Crème Fraîche (page 110) or Whipped Cream (page 109).*

MAKES 12 SERVINGS.

*P*osition racks so that the cake will bake in the middle of an oven and preheat the oven to 350° F. Grease a 13-by-9-inch pan as directed on page 15; do not line or flour it. Set aside.

Toast the pecans as directed on page 123, then chop and set aside.

Place the flour, sugar, cocoa, baking soda, and salt together in a strainer or sifter and sift into a bowl. Whisk to mix well. Add 2 cups water, the oil, vinegar, and vanilla, and whisk or beat with an electric mixer just until the ingredients are well blended.

Scrape 3 cups of the batter into the prepared pan and smooth the surface with a rubber spatula. Bake until the top is just set, about 15 minutes.

Remove the pan to a work surface. Sprinkle the chocolate chips and toasted pecans evenly over the partially baked cake, then drizzle evenly with the Caramel Sauce. Cover with the remaining cake batter and smooth the surface. Bake until the cake feels firm when lightly touched in the center with your fingertip and a skewer inserted into the center of the cake comes out moist but not gooey, about 35 minutes longer.

Remove the pan to a wire rack to cool completely.

Cut into narrow slices, as shown in the photograph, or squares and serve directly from the pan.

1 cup pecans

3 cups all-purpose flour

2 cups sugar

$1/2$ cup unsweetened natural cocoa (not Dutch-processed)

2 teaspoons baking soda

1 teaspoon salt

$3/4$ cup canola or other high-quality vegetable oil

2 tablespoons distilled white or cider vinegar

2 teaspoons pure vanilla extract

1 cup chopped finest-quality semisweet chocolate or chocolate chips

$1^1/2$ cups Caramel Sauce (page 122) or high-quality commercial caramel or butterscotch sauce

Molten Chocolate Babycakes

This version of the popular individual warm chocolate cakes is the result of ideas gleaned from pastry chefs from coast to coast. To insure that the fudgy centers are runny, time the preparation of the cakes so they can be served hot from the oven. Or bake them up to a day ahead, cool, cover, and store at room temperature; reheat uncovered in a 350° F oven for about 10 minutes or in a microwave oven at full power for about 25 seconds, being careful not to cook the cakes further when reheating. ❊ *Tissue-thin sheets of gold leaf make a luxurious garnish and reinforce the suggestion of flowing molten lava from the little mounds of cake. The inert metal is edible and may be purchased at art-supply stores and some cake decorating supply stores.* ❊ *Instead of the suggested custard sauce, consider serving the cakes with Fresh Berry Sauce (page 123), Caramel Sauce (page 122), Chocolate Sauce (page 121) made with white chocolate, or Whipped Cream (page 109).*

MAKES 6 SERVINGS.

Prepare the Crème Anglaise and refrigerate as directed until serving.

Position racks so that the cakes will bake in the middle of an oven and preheat the oven to 400° F. Grease and line six 6-ounce custard cups or soufflé dishes as directed on page 14. Set aside.

Melt the chocolate as directed on page 125 and set aside to cool slightly.

In a bowl or food processor, combine the butter, granulated sugar, salt, and eggs and beat with an electric mixer at medium speed or process until well blended. Add the flour and blend well. Add the vanilla and cooled chocolate and blend until smooth.

Divide the batter evenly among the prepared baking dishes and smooth the surfaces with a small rubber spatula. Place on a baking sheet, transfer to the oven, and bake until the tops are well puffed, about 17 minutes.

Remove the baking dishes to a wire rack to cool for about 5 minutes, then run a thin knife blade around the sides of each cake and invert directly onto individual serving plates. Peel off the parchment. Top each cake with a sheet of gold leaf (if using) or lightly sift a little powdered sugar over the tops of the cakes. Spoon a portion of the Crème Anglaise around each cake, then add dollops of mango and raspberry purees (if using) and swirl with a wooden skewer.

Crème Anglaise (page 120)

12 ounces finest-quality bittersweet (not unsweetened) or semisweet chocolate, finely chopped

3 tablespoons unsalted butter, at room temperature

$^2/_3$ cup granulated sugar

$^1/_8$ teaspoon salt

4 eggs, at room temperature, lightly beaten

$^1/_2$ cup cake flour

1 teaspoon pure vanilla extract

Gold leaf for garnish (see recipe introduction; optional)

Powdered sugar for dusting, if not using gold leaf

Mango and raspberry purees for swirling (optional)

Coffee Crunch Cake

Longtime San Franciscans still speak nostalgically of Koffee Krunch Cake as sold at the long-departed Blum's on Union Square. Although the store closed about the time of my arrival in The City in the mid-1970s, my "sister" Kristi Cotton Spence first told me about the cake and shared the recipe. ❧ The crunch is best made and used on a dry day, as high humidity will cause it to "weep." Refrigeration will bring about the same effect, so plan to enjoy the whole cake soon after assembling. ❧ For a nontraditional version, substitute Coffee Chiffon Cake (page 43) for the sponge cake.

MAKES 12 SERVINGS.

To make the Coffee Crunch, in a very deep, heavy saucepan, combine the sugar, coffee or dissolved espresso, and corn syrup. Place over medium-low heat and stir frequently until the sugar is dissolved, then increase the heat to medium-high and cook until the mixture registers between 270° and 290° F (soft-crack stage) on a candy thermometer. Toward the end of cooking, stir almost constantly to prevent the mixture from scorching. Remove from the heat and quickly stir in the baking soda; the mixture will foam furiously. Stir rapidly just until the mixture thickens and pulls away from the sides of the pan; do not stir down the foam. Quickly pour onto an ungreased baking sheet; do not spread. Set aside to cool completely until hard, about 1 hour.

Knock the hardened crunch off the baking sheet, break into chunks, then pound with a blunt instrument or cut with kitchen scissors to create small irregular pieces. Place in an airtight container and store in a cool, dry place for up to 3 days.

Make and cool the American Sponge Cake as directed.

Prepare the Whipped Cream Frosting as directed. Slice the cake horizontally into 3 layers as directed on page 18. Fill and frost the cake as directed on pages 18–19 and refrigerate for up to 24 hours.

Just before serving, remove the cake from the refrigerator and lavishly cover the sides and top with the Coffee Crunch pieces.

COFFEE CRUNCH

1 1/2 cups sugar

1/4 cup strong brewed coffee, or 1 teaspoon instant espresso dissolved in 1/4 cup hot water

1/4 cup light corn syrup

1 tablespoon baking soda, sifted

American Sponge Cake (page 36)
Whipped Cream Frosting (page 109)

Poppy Seed Cake

Mary Val McCoy introduced me to her family's special-occasion cake. Although the McCoy clan frosts their version with chocolate,
Mary shrieked with joy when I suggested crowning the cake with white chocolate ganache to complement the deep purple poppy seeds.

MAKES 12 SERVINGS.

$^3/_4$ *cup poppy seeds (about 4 ounces)*

1 cup whole milk

1 cup egg whites (from about 8 eggs), at
*   room temperature*

2 teaspoons pure vanilla extract

3 cups all-purpose flour

1 tablespoon baking powder

$^3/_4$ *teaspoon salt*

2 cups sugar

1 cup (2 sticks) unsalted butter, at room
*   temperature*

Custard Filling (page 106)

Ganache (page 117) made with white
*   chocolate*

Poppy seeds for sprinkling

In a bowl or measuring cup, combine the $^3/_4$ cup poppy seeds and milk and let stand for about 1 hour to soften the seeds.

Position racks so that the cake layers will bake in the middle of an oven and preheat the oven to 350° F. Grease and line two 9-inch cake pans as directed on page 14. Set aside.

Add the egg whites and vanilla to the poppy seed mixture and whisk to blend well. Set aside.

Place the flour, baking powder, and salt together in a strainer or sifter and sift into a bowl. Add the sugar and mix with an electric mixer at low speed until well blended, about 30 seconds. Add the butter and beat at medium speed until the mixture resembles coarse bread crumbs, about 45 seconds. Add about $^3/_4$ cup of the poppy seed mixture and beat at medium speed if using a stand mixer or high speed if using a hand mixer for 1$^1/_2$ minutes, then stop the mixer and scrape the mixture that clings to the sides of the bowl into the center. Add the remaining poppy seed mixture and beat at the same speed for 30 seconds, then stop and scrape down the sides of the bowl and beat again until the mixture is creamy smooth, about 30 seconds.

Divide the batter evenly between the prepared pans and smooth the surfaces with a rubber spatula. Bake until each cake layer springs back when lightly touched in the center with your fingertip and a wooden skewer inserted into the center of each layer comes out clean, about 30 minutes.

Remove the pans to a wire rack to cool for 5 to 10 minutes, then turn the layers out onto the rack to cool completely as directed on page 17.

Prepare the Custard Filling and Ganache as directed. Slice each cake layer horizontally in half to create 4 layers total as directed on page 18. Fill the layers with the Custard Filling and frost the top and sides of the cake with the Ganache as directed on pages 18–19. Lightly sprinkle poppy seeds over the top.

Cherry Spice Cake

My mother always made this cake for my birthday, and still makes it for me whenever I visit Louisiana in the fall or winter. She got the recipe from my paternal grandmother, Mary Izetta Woods McNair. It's the only good use that I know of for bottled maraschino cherries. ✽ All of the cooks in my family fill and frost this cake with cooked caramel frosting, which is fabulous but can prove tricky for the caramel-making novice. An easy, satisfying alternative is Butterscotch Frosting (page 119). Butterscotch Buttercream (page 112), shown in the photograph, is a light-tasting yet luxurious option. ✽ As this old-fashioned cake becomes more flavorful and moist when left to stand at room temperature, make it a day or two before serving. If you finish the cake with buttercream, wrap the cooled layers tightly for storage, then frost shortly before serving.

MAKES 12 SERVINGS.

1 cup pecans

About 18 perfect pecan halves

2 cups all-purpose flour

1 cup cake flour

1 tablespoon baking powder

1 teaspoon salt

1 teaspoon ground cinnamon

1 teaspoon ground cloves

1 cup (2 sticks) unsalted butter, at room temperature

2 cups sugar

4 eggs, at room temperature, lightly beaten

1 cup applesauce, at room temperature

1 cup finely chopped drained maraschino cherries

2 teaspoons pure vanilla extract

1 cup buttermilk, at room temperature

Old-fashioned Caramel Frosting (page 118)

About 18 drained maraschino, candied, or glazed (glacéed) cherries for garnish

Position racks so that the cake layers will bake in the middle of an oven and preheat the oven to 350° F. Grease and line three or four 9-inch round cake pans as directed on page 14. Set aside.

In 2 separate pans, toast the pecans as directed on page 123. Set the halves aside to use as garnish. Chop the 1 cup pecans finely and set aside.

Place the flours, baking powder, salt, cinnamon, and cloves together in a strainer or sifter and sift into a bowl. Repeat the process two more times. Whisk to mix well and set aside.

In the bowl of a stand mixer fitted with a flat beater, or in a bowl with a hand mixer, beat the butter at medium speed until soft and creamy, about 45 seconds. With the mixer still running, slowly add the sugar, then stop the mixer and scrape the mixture that clings to the sides of the bowl into the center. Continue beating at medium speed until very light and fluffy, about 5 minutes. Slowly drizzle in the eggs and beat well; stop at least once to scrape the sides of the bowl. Add the applesauce, chopped cherries, and vanilla and blend well.

Using the mixer on low speed or a rubber spatula, fold in about one-third of the flour mixture, then half of the buttermilk, scraping the sides of the bowl and folding just until the ingredients are incorporated. In the same manner, fold in half of the remaining flour mixture, then the remaining buttermilk, and finally the remaining flour mixture. Fold in the chopped nuts.

Divide the batter evenly between the prepared pans and smooth the surfaces with a rubber spatula. Bake until each cake layer springs back when touched in the center with your fingertip and a wooden skewer inserted into the center of each layer comes out clean, about 25 minutes if using 4 pans, or about 30 minutes if using three pans.

Remove the pans to a wire rack to cool for 5 to 10 minutes, then turn the layers out onto the rack to cool completely as directed on page 17.

Prepare the Old-fashioned Caramel Frosting as directed. Fill and frost the cake as directed on pages 18–19. Arrange the toasted pecan halves and whole cherries around the perimeter of the top.

Nut Cake

Having grown up in a Louisiana town surrounded by acres of pecan trees, I favor these wonderful nuts for this recipe that dates back to the Old South. It is also fabulous and a beautiful golden yellow when made with blanched almonds. Feel free to use your favorite nut or a mixture. The cake is delicious plain warm from the oven or simply adorned with dollops of Whipped Cream (page 109) and/or Chocolate Sauce (page 121) or Caramel Sauce (page 122). To create a more festive cake, glaze with Chocolate or Coffee Glaze (pages 104–105).

MAKES 8 SERVINGS.

Position racks so that the cake will bake in the middle of an oven and preheat the oven to 350° F. Grease and line a 9-inch springform pan as directed on page 14. Set aside.

In a food processor, combine the nuts and ¾ cup of the sugar and pulverize to form a fine meal. Set aside.

Place the flour, baking powder, and salt together in a strainer or sifter and sift into a bowl. Add the ground nut mixture, whisk to mix well, and set aside.

In the bowl of a stand mixer fitted with a flat beater, or in a bowl with a hand mixer, beat the butter at medium speed until soft and creamy, about 45 seconds. With the mixer still running, slowly add the remaining ¾ cup sugar and the orange zest (if using), then stop the mixer and scrape the mixture that clings to the sides of the bowl into the center. Continue beating at medium speed until the mixture is very light and fluffy, about 5 minutes. Slowly drizzle in the eggs and beat well; stop at least once to scrape the sides of the bowl. Add the cream or half-and-half and vanilla and almond extracts and blend well.

Using the mixer on low speed or a rubber spatula, fold in the nut mixture.

Using a rubber spatula, scrape the batter into the prepared pan. Bake until the cake springs back when lightly touched in the center with your fingertip and a wooden skewer inserted into the center of the cake comes out clean, about 40 minutes.

Remove the pan to a wire rack to cool for 5 to 10 minutes, then turn the cake out onto the rack to cool completely as directed on page 17.

Transfer the cake to a serving plate and dust the top with powdered sugar. If desired, cover the cake with a stencil before dusting with powdered sugar, then carefully remove the stencil.

1½ cups almonds, pecans, or other nuts

1½ cups sugar

¾ cup all-purpose flour

1 teaspoon baking powder

½ teaspoon salt

½ cup (1 stick) unsalted butter, at room temperature

1 tablespoon grated or minced fresh orange zest (optional)

5 eggs, at room temperature, lightly beaten

½ cup light cream or half-and-half, at room temperature

2 teaspoons pure vanilla extract

1 teaspoon pure almond extract

Powdered sugar for dusting

Orange Date-Nut Cake

Although I never learned why, the two Episcopal priests who served me this rich cake many years ago called it Horse Show Cake. By any name, it is an excellent treat with tea or coffee. Oil your kitchen scissors to make snipping the sticky dates easier.

MAKES 10 SERVINGS.

$1\frac{1}{2}$ *cups chopped or snipped high-quality dates, preferably plump Medjool variety*

1 cup chopped pecans

2 cups all-purpose flour

$\frac{1}{2}$ *teaspoon baking soda*

$\frac{1}{2}$ *teaspoon salt*

1 cup (2 sticks) unsalted butter, at room temperature

1 cup sugar

2 tablespoons grated or minced fresh orange zest

2 eggs, at room temperature, lightly beaten

1 teaspoon pure vanilla extract

1 teaspoon pure orange extract

1 cup buttermilk, at room temperature

Citrus Glaze (page 104) made with orange juice and zest

Position racks so that the cake will bake in the middle of an oven and preheat the oven to 350° F. Grease and line a 9-by-5-inch loaf pan as directed on page 14.

In a bowl, combine the dates, pecans, and $\frac{1}{2}$ cup of the flour and toss well to coat the nuts and dates; set aside. (This step helps to keep these ingredients suspended throughout the cake during baking.)

Place the remaining $1\frac{1}{2}$ cups flour, the baking soda, and salt together in a strainer or sifter and sift into a bowl. Repeat the process two more times. Whisk to mix well and set aside.

In the bowl of a stand mixer fitted with a flat beater, or in a bowl with a hand mixer, beat the butter at medium speed until soft and creamy, about 45 seconds. With the mixer still running, slowly add the sugar, then stop the mixer and scrape the mixture that clings to the sides of the bowl into the center. Add the orange zest and continue beating until the mixture is very light and fluffy, about 5 minutes. Slowly drizzle in the eggs and beat well; stop at least once to scrape the sides of the bowl. Add the vanilla and orange extracts and blend well.

Using the mixer on low speed or a rubber spatula, fold in about one-third of the flour mixture, then half of the buttermilk, scraping the sides of the bowl and folding just until the ingredients are incorporated. In the same manner, fold in half of the remaining flour mixture, then the remaining buttermilk, and finally the remaining flour mixture. Stir in the date-nut mixture.

Scrape the batter into the prepared pan and smooth the surface with a rubber spatula. Bake until the cake springs back when lightly touched in the center with your fingertip and a wooden skewer inserted into the center of the cake comes out clean, about $1\frac{1}{4}$ hours; if the top begins to brown too quickly during baking, cover loosely with aluminum foil.

Remove the pan to a wire rack to cool for 5 to 10 minutes. Meanwhile, prepare the Citrus Glaze as directed.

Turn the cake out onto the rack as directed on page 17. Place the most attractive side up and pierce the top all over with a wooden skewer. Brush some of the glaze on the sides and top of the warm cake, then spoon the remaining glaze over the cake until it is all used. Let the cake cool completely.

Dundee Cake

Perhaps it is my Scottish heritage that makes this traditional cake so enjoyable with my afternoon tea. The dry cake is complemented by dollops of imported English clotted cream, Crème Fraîche (page 110), or commercial crème fraîche.

MAKES 12 SERVINGS.

Position racks so that the cake will bake in the middle of an oven and preheat the oven to 325° F. Grease and line a 9-inch springform pan as directed on page 14. Set aside.

In a bowl, combine the currants, raisins, candied zest, and chopped almonds. Add $^1/_4$ cup of the flour and stir to coat the fruits and nuts well with the flour; set aside. (This step helps to keep these ingredients suspended throughout the cake during baking.)

Place the remaining 2 cups flour, the baking powder, and salt together in a strainer or sifter and sift into a bowl. Repeat the process two more times. Whisk to mix well and set aside.

In the bowl of a stand mixer fitted with a flat beater, or in a bowl with a hand mixer, beat the butter at medium speed until soft and creamy, about 45 seconds. With the mixer still running, slowly add the sugar, then stop the mixer and scrape the mixture that clings to the sides of the bowl into the center. Add the fresh lemon and orange zest and continue beating at medium speed until the mixture is very light and fluffy, about 5 minutes. Slowly drizzle in the eggs and beat well; stop at least once to scrape the sides of the bowl. Add the vanilla and almond extracts and blend well.

Using the mixer on low speed or a rubber spatula, fold in the flour mixture in 3 equal batches until well incorporated. Fold in the fruit-and-nut mixture until well incorporated.

Scrape the batter into the prepared pan and smooth the surface with a rubber spatula. Arrange whole almonds and cherry halves in a decorative pattern over the top. Bake until the cake springs back when lightly touched in the center with your fingertip and a wooden skewer inserted into the center of the cake comes out clean, about $1^1/_4$ hours.

Remove the pan to a wire rack to cool for about 10 minutes, then turn the cake out onto the rack to cool completely as directed on page 17.

1 cup dried currants

1 cup golden raisins

$^3/_4$ cup chopped Candied Orange Zest (page 127) or high-quality commercial candied citrus zest

$^1/_2$ cup finely chopped blanched or raw almonds

$2^1/_4$ cups all-purpose flour

1 teaspoon baking powder

$^1/_2$ teaspoon salt

1 cup (2 sticks) unsalted butter, at room temperature

1 cup sugar

$1^1/_2$ tablespoons grated or minced fresh lemon zest

$1^1/_2$ tablespoons grated or minced fresh orange zest

4 eggs, at room temperature, lightly beaten

1 teaspoon pure vanilla extract

1 teaspoon pure almond extract

Whole blanched almonds for decorating

Candied or glazed (glacéed) cherries, halved, for decorating

Royal Gingerbread

My partner, Andrew, perfected this recipe and suggested the Victorian presentation and name in honor of the drizzle of Royal Icing and the rich blend of winter spices. He often divides the batter among individual-sized (1-cup) fluted tube pans to make baby cakes, which bake in about 25 minutes. ❀ My favorite gingerbread presentation is to use a 13-by-9-inch pan, which bakes in about 45 minutes. I serve squares of the warm cake from the pan with Old-fashioned Dessert Sauce (page 123). For a smaller cake, cut the recipe in half and bake in an 8-inch square pan, which should be done in about 35 minutes. ❀ For an unusual layer cake, divide the batter between two 9-inch round cake pans, bake for about 30 minutes, and fill and frost with vanilla-flavored Buttercream (page 112), Cream Cheese Frosting (page 111), or Ganache (page 117).

MAKES 12 SERVINGS.

3 cups all-purpose flour

2 teaspoons baking powder

$1/4$ teaspoon baking soda

1 teaspoon salt

1 tablespoon ground ginger

2 teaspoons ground cinnamon

$1^1/_2$ teaspoons finely ground black or white pepper

1 teaspoon ground allspice

1 teaspoon ground cloves

1 teaspoon freshly grated nutmeg

2 cups sugar

$1/2$ cup dark molasses

1 cup (2 sticks) unsalted butter, melted and cooled slightly

1 cup whole milk, at room temperature

2 eggs, at room temperature

Royal Icing (page 120; for using as a glaze) or Citrus Glaze (page 104) made with lemon juice and zest

Silver and/or jewel-toned metallic dragées (optional)

Position racks so that the cake will bake in the middle of an oven and preheat the oven to 350° F. Grease and flour a 10-inch Bundt or other fluted tube pan as directed on page 14. Set aside.

Place the flour, baking powder, baking soda, salt, ginger, cinnamon, pepper, allspice, cloves, and nutmeg together in a strainer or sifter and sift into a bowl. Whisk to mix well and set aside.

In a bowl, combine the sugar, molasses, butter, milk, and eggs and beat with an electric mixer at medium speed until smooth, about 1 minute.

Using the mixer on low speed or a rubber spatula, fold in the flour mixture just until incorporated.

Scrape the batter into the prepared pan and smooth the surface with a rubber spatula. Bake until the cake springs back when lightly touched in the thickest part with your fingertip and a wooden skewer inserted into the thickest part of the cake comes out clean, about 1 hour.

Remove the pan to a wire rack to cool for 5 to 10 minutes, then turn the cake out onto the rack as directed on page 17.

Prepare the Royal Icing or Citrus Glaze as directed and spoon it over the top of the cake, allowing some to drizzle down the sides. Quickly arrange the dragées (if using) on top and serve warm or at room temperature.

Winter Fruitcake

Finishes

Whether you call it frosting or icing depends on where you live and your own family tradition. No matter which you prefer, it can transform an ordinary cake into a magnificent treat. Fillings between layers add something special, too. Some cakes are enhanced by a luscious sauce, perfectly whipped cream, or tangy crème fraîche. I've also included a few tasty garnishes to turn even the simplest cake into a celebration.

The amount of filling and/or frosting needed varies with its richness, how thick you like to pile it on, and the size of the cake. You may wish to increase or divide recipes according to preference. As a general guide, a 9-inch cake takes $\frac{1}{2}$ to 1 cup filling or frosting between each layer, 1 to $1\frac{1}{2}$ cups frosting to cover the top, and $\frac{1}{2}$ to 1 cup frosting to coat the sides of each layer.

The following list should help you plan the quantity needed to fill and frost most cakes; lean toward the smaller amount for denser, more intensely flavored mixtures and the larger amount for lighter, fluffier ones (you'll need even more for multilayer or larger cakes, of course). Just don't skimp on the volume you prepare, as it is frustrating to run out of frosting or filling before your creation is finished. Also, having a little extra on hand is helpful when last-minute repairs are necessary. And most leftovers can be stored for another use (like midnight snacks).

9-inch single-layer cake: $1\frac{1}{2}$ to $2\frac{1}{2}$ cups to cover the top and sides.

9-inch two-layer cake: $\frac{1}{2}$ to 1 cup to fill, plus 2 to 3 cups to cover the top and sides.

9-inch three-layer cake: 1 to 2 cups to fill, plus $2\frac{1}{2}$ to 4 cups to cover the top and sides.

10-inch tube cake: $2\frac{1}{2}$ to 3 cups to cover the top and sides.

10-inch tube cake split into layers: $\frac{1}{2}$ to 1 cup between each layer, plus 3 to 4 cups to cover the top and sides.

13-by-9-inch single-layer cake: $1\frac{1}{2}$ to 2 cups to cover the top, or $2\frac{1}{2}$ to 3 cups to cover the top and sides

13-by-9-inch two-layer cake: $1\frac{1}{2}$ to 2 cups to fill, plus 3 to 4 cups to cover the top and sides.

Glazes

Some cakes need only a simple glaze to finish them. Add enough liquid to create a mixture that is creamy and smooth and pourable but not too thin. Most glazes must be used as soon as they are made, as they set up quickly. ❊ *See page 17 for directions on how to finish cakes with glazes*

EACH GLAZE MAKES ENOUGH TO COVER THINLY THE TOP AND SIDES OF A 9-OR 10-INCH CAKE.

Chocolate Glaze

For cakes that will not be refrigerated, finely chop 6 ounces finest-quality semisweet or bittersweet (not unsweetened) chocolate and place in a heatproof bowl. Add $\frac{1}{2}$ cup (1 stick) unsalted butter and 1 tablespoon light corn syrup. **For cakes that will be chilled,** finely chop 8 ounces finest-quality semisweet or bittersweet (not unsweetened) chocolate and place in a heatproof bowl. Add $\frac{3}{4}$ cup ($1\frac{1}{2}$ sticks) unsalted butter, 2 tablespoons water, and 1 tablespoon light corn syrup. **For either glaze,** set the bowl in a skillet or shallow saucepan containing about 1 inch of barely simmering water and stir the chocolate mixture gently until almost completely melted. Remove from the heat and stir gently just until smooth; do not beat. Let cool slightly before pouring over a completely cooled cake. Refrigerate the chilled version immediately.

Citrus Glaze

Sift 2 cups powdered sugar into a bowl. Add 2 tablespoons unsalted butter, melted, and a pinch of salt. Gradually stir in enough freshly squeezed lemon, lime, orange, or tangerine juice (about 6 tablespoons) to create a smooth, pourable mixture. Stir in 1 tablespoon finely grated or minced fresh zest of same fruit as the juice. Use immediately.

Cocoa Glaze

Sift 1½ cups powdered sugar and ½ cup unsweetened cocoa, preferably Dutch-processed (alkalized), into a bowl. Add 1 tablespoon unsalted butter, melted. Gradually stir in 1 teaspoon pure vanilla extract and just enough warm milk or boiling water (about ¼ cup) to create a smooth, pourable mixture. Use immediately.

Coffee Glaze

Sift 2 cups powdered sugar into a bowl. Add 1 tablespoon unsalted butter, melted. Dissolve 1 tablespoon instant espresso in ¼ cup hot water or ready ¼ cup hot strong brewed coffee. Gradually stir just enough of the espresso or coffee into the sugar to create a smooth, pourable mixture. Use immediately.

Guava or Passion Fruit Glaze

Sift 2 cups powdered sugar into a bowl. Add 1 tablespoon melted unsalted butter. Gradually stir in just enough fresh or thawed frozen guava pulp or passion fruit juice or thawed frozen juice concentrate (about ¼ cup) to create a smooth, pourable mixture. Use immediately.

Jam or Jelly Glaze

In a small saucepan over medium heat, melt 1½ cups apricot or other fruit jam or jelly until melted and pourable. If using jam, pour through a strainer and discard fruit pieces and/or seeds. Use immediately.

Sparkling Sugar Glaze

Combine ¾ cup sugar with ⅓ cup freshly squeezed lemon, lime, orange, or tangerine juice, or a combination of juices, and stir to blend well. Brush over a warm cake, using all of the glaze. Cool completely; the juice will soak into the cake, leaving sparkling crystals of sugar on the surface.

Spirited Glaze

Sift 2 cups powdered sugar into a bowl. Add 1 tablespoon unsalted butter, melted. Gradually stir in just enough rum, bourbon, liqueur, or other favorite spirit (about ¼ cup) to create a smooth, pourable mixture. Use immediately.

Vanilla Glaze

Sift 2 cups powdered sugar into a bowl. Add 1 tablespoon unsalted butter, melted. Gradually stir in 1 teaspoon pure vanilla extract and just enough warm milk or boiling water (about ¼ cup) to create a smooth, pourable mixture. Use immediately.

White Chocolate Glaze

Finely chop 10 ounces finest-quality white chocolate containing cocoa butter and place in a bowl. In a saucepan, combine ½ cup heavy (whipping) cream and 1 tablespoon light corn syrup and bring to a simmer over medium heat. Pour the mixture over the white chocolate and stir gently until completely melted and smooth. Let cool slightly before pouring over a cake. Can also be made ahead and slowly reheated just before using.

Lemon or Lime Curd

This British classic not only makes a decadent filling for a layer cake, but is also marvelous spread on toasted slices of stale pound cake. For a lighter curd texture, substitute 2 whole eggs for an equal number of yolks. If using Meyer lemons, reduce the sugar to 1 cup. ❄ *I prefer curd without flecks of zest, so I strain the zest out after it contributes its zing. If you wish, wait and add the zest after the curd is strained.*

M A K E S   A B O U T   2$^1/_2$ C U P S .

6 egg yolks
1$^1/_4$ cups sugar
Pinch of salt
$^3/_4$ cup freshly squeezed lemon or lime juice
1$^1/_2$ tablespoons grated or minced fresh lemon or lime zest
$^1/_2$ cup (1 stick) unsalted butter, cut into small pieces

*I*n a heavy nonreactive pan, such as stainless steel, combine the egg yolks, sugar, and salt and beat until light and well blended. Stir in the lemon or lime juice and zest. Add the butter, place over medium-low heat, and cook, stirring and scraping the bottom of the pan constantly, until the mixture is thick enough to coat the back of a spoon (your finger should leave a trail when you run it across the spoon) but remains pourable, 5 to 10 minutes. To prevent the eggs from curdling, do not allow the mixture to approach a boil.

Pour the curd through a fine-mesh strainer into a bowl. Immediately place a piece of plastic wrap directly onto the surface of the curd to prevent a skin from forming. Set aside to cool completely, then discard the plastic wrap, cover tightly, and refrigerate for up to 3 weeks.

VARIATIONS

Orange or Tangerine Curd

In a saucepan, place 1 cup freshly squeezed orange or tangerine juice over medium heat and cook until the juice is reduced to $^1/_4$ cup, then set aside to cool to room temperature. Make the curd as directed, reducing the sugar to $^1/_2$ cup and substituting the reduced orange or tangerine juice for the lemon or lime juice and 2 tablespoons orange zest for the lemon or lime zest. Makes about 1$^1/_2$ cups.

Passion Fruit Curd

Reduce the sugar to 1 cup. Substitute fresh or thawed frozen passion fruit juice for the lemon or lime juice. Omit the zest.

Creamy Curd Frosting

Any of the preceding curds can be used to create this tangy, cloud-light spread. Please read about choosing the best type of cream for whipping on page 11.

M A K E S   A B O U T   5   C U P S .

1 cup Lemon or Lime Curd (left) or any variation
1 envelope (2$^1/_2$ teaspoons) unflavored gelatin
2 cups heavy (whipping) cream, preferably not ultrapasteurized, well chilled
About 2 tablespoons powdered sugar

*P*lace a metal bowl and a wire whisk or the beaters of a hand mixer in a freezer until well chilled.

In a small heatproof bowl, combine $1/2$ cup of the curd and the gelatin, stir well, and set aside to soften for about 5 minutes.

In a skillet, pour in water to a depth of 1 inch, place over medium heat, bring just to a simmer, and adjust the heat to maintain barely simmering water. Place the bowl of gelatin mixture in the simmering water and stir the mixture constantly until the gelatin is dissolved. Remove from the water, add the remaining $1/2$ cup curd, stir to blend well, and set aside to cool slightly.

Pour the cream into the chilled bowl. Beat with the chilled whisk or hand mixer just until the cream begins to thicken. Add the curd mixture and 2 tablespoons sugar and beat just until stiff peaks form when the beater is raised. Taste and blend in more sugar if desired. Use immediately.

Whipped Cream

Please read about choosing the best type of cream for whipping on page 11. ❀ For serving with cake, create crème chantilly by whipping the cream just until it holds its shape. For folding into a frosting, whip the cream a little stiffer, but avoid overbeating. The cornstarch present in powdered sugar helps stabilize whipped cream.

MAKES ABOUT 2 CUPS, FOR 8 SERVINGS.

1 cup heavy (whipping) cream, preferably not ultrapasteurized, well chilled
About 2 tablespoons granulated sugar or powdered sugar
$1/2$ teaspoon pure vanilla extract

Place a metal bowl and a wire whisk or the beaters of a hand mixer in a freezer until well chilled.

Pour the cream into the chilled bowl. Beat with the chilled

whisk or hand mixer just until the cream begins to thicken. Add the sugar and vanilla and continue to beat to the desired stage (please see recipe introduction); be very careful not to overbeat if using a hand mixer (you may wish to finish the whipping by hand with a whisk). Use immediately.

Whipped Cream Frosting

I'm indebted to Rose Levy Beranbaum's marvelous book, The Cake Bible, *for the idea for this voluptuous version of whipped cream. The cream holds up on a cake for several hours at room temperature or for up to 2 days in a refrigerator. Please read about choosing the best type of cream for whipping on page 11.*

MAKES ABOUT 4 CUPS.

$1/4$ cup powdered sugar
$2 1/2$ teaspoons cornstarch
2 cups heavy (whipping) cream, preferably not ultrapasteurized, well chilled
1 teaspoon pure vanilla extract

Place a metal bowl and a wire whisk or the beaters of a hand mixer in a freezer until well chilled.

In a small saucepan, combine the powdered sugar and cornstarch and whisk to mix well. Slowly whisk in $1/2$ cup of the cream until smooth. Place over medium heat and stir constantly to prevent scorching on the bottom until the mixture just begins to thicken and comes almost to a boil. Transfer to a bowl and set aside, stirring occasionally, to cool to room temperature.

In the chilled bowl, combine the remaining $1 1/2$ cups cream and the vanilla and beat with the chilled whisk or hand mixer ➤

just until tl
add the poʋ
until the m
is spreadabl

During sto
that is sligh.
now sel.
If you

MAH

2 cups h
1/4 cup b.

𝒥n a saucep
over low hea
85° to 95° F
Pour th
tially, and se
spoonable co
eral hours on
Stir the
for at least 24
to thicken d
liquid that se

Royal Icing

If the eggs in your area cause concern about problems with salmonella, use meringue powder in this recipe. This stiff icing is generally used for adding decorative touches to cakes. The thinner version works well as a decorative glaze for gingerbread or other dense cakes.

MAKES ABOUT 3/4 CUP.

1 tablespoon meringue powder (available from cake-decorating
  supply stores), or 1 egg white, at room temperature
1 1/2 cups powdered sugar, sifted if necessary to remove lumps
1 tablespoon freshly squeezed lemon juice (if using as a glaze)
Food coloring (optional)

𝒥f using meringue powder, in a bowl, combine the meringue powder and 2 tablespoons water, stir well, and set aside to soak for 30 minutes.

In a bowl, combine the egg white or soaked meringue powder and sugar and beat with a hand mixer at low speed until blended.

If *using as a glaze,* add the lemon juice, increase the mixer speed to high, and beat until creamy and shiny, about 2 minutes. Add enough food coloring (if using) to achieve desired color. Quickly pour or spoon the glaze over the cake.

If *using for decorations or writing,* increase the mixer speed to high and beat until stiff, very shiny peaks form when the beater is lifted, about 6 minutes. Add enough food coloring (if using) to achieve desired color, or divide the icing among small bowls and tint with various colors as desired. Spoon some of the icing into a pastry bag and use immediately for decorating or writing; cover bowl(s) of remaining icing with a damp cloth to keep from drying out.

Crème Anglaise

If you can resist just sitting down and eating this creamy custard sauce with a spoon, serve it with almost any cake, especially chocolate, spice, or gingerbread.

MAKES ABOUT 2 CUPS, FOR 8 SERVINGS.

2 cups whole milk or half-and-half
1 vanilla bean, split lengthwise (optional)
5 egg yolks, at room temperature
1/2 cup sugar
Pinch of salt
2 teaspoons pure vanilla extract (if not using a vanilla bean)

𝒥n a heavy saucepan, combine the milk or half-and-half and vanilla bean (if using). Place over medium heat and bring almost to the boiling point, then remove from the heat. If using a vanilla bean, using the tip of a small, sharp knife, scrape the seeds into the milk and stir to combine; discard the bean.

In another heavy saucepan, combine the egg yolks, sugar, and salt and whisk until creamy. Gradually whisk in the hot milk or half-and-half. Place over low heat and cook, stirring constantly, just until the mixture is thick enough to coat the back of a spoon (your finger should leave a trail when you run it across the spoon), about 5 minutes. To prevent the eggs from overcooking or curdling, do not allow the mixture to approach a boil.

Pour the mixture through a fine-mesh strainer into a bowl. If not using a vanilla bean, stir the vanilla extract into the sauce.

Serve warm, or set aside to cool to room temperature, stirring frequently to prevent a skin from forming on the surface. Cover and refrigerate until well chilled, at least 4 hours or for up to 3 days.

VARIATIONS

Chocolate Crème Anglaise

Use the vanilla extract instead of the vanilla bean. Grate or finely chop 2 ounces finest-quality bittersweet (not unsweetened), semi-sweet, milk, or white chocolate containing cocoa butter, add to the warm finished sauce, and stir until the chocolate is melted and well blended.

Coconut Crème Anglaise

Substitute Fresh Coconut Milk (page 124) or high-quality commercial coconut milk for the milk or half-and-half.

Coffee Crème Anglaise

Stir 2 tablespoons instant espresso, or to taste, into the hot milk or half-and-half.

Lemon Crème Anglaise

Add 2 tablespoons grated or minced fresh lemon zest to the milk or half-and-half along with only $1/2$ of the vanilla bean (if using) before heating; if using vanilla extract, use only 1 teaspoon.

Nut Crème Anglaise

In a saucepan, melt 2 tablespoons unsalted butter over medium-low heat. Add 1 cup chopped almonds, cashews, pistachios, or other nuts and cook, stirring frequently, until the nuts are lightly browned and fragrant, about 5 minutes. Stir in 1 cup whole milk or half-and-half, reduce the heat to achieve a simmer, and simmer for about 30 minutes. Pour the milk or half-and-half through a strainer into a measuring cup; discard the nuts. Add enough whole milk or half-and-half to equal 2 cups and prepare the sauce as directed.

Orange Crème Anglaise

Reduce the amount of milk or half-and-half to $1/2$ cups and add 2 tablespoons grated or minced fresh orange zest along with only $1/2$ of the vanilla bean (if using) before heating; if using vanilla extract, use only 1 teaspoon. When adding the half-and-half to the egg mixture, stir in $1/2$ cup freshly squeezed orange juice.

Spirited Crème Anglaise

Stir 1 tablespoon of a favorite liqueur into the finished sauce

Chocolate Sauce

Start with the finest chocolate you can buy for this all-purpose sauce for angel food, pound, or other plain cakes. Instead of the vanilla, flavor the sauce with a liqueur such as raspberry-flavored Chambord, hazelnut-flavored Frangelico, orange-flavored Grand Marnier, or coffee-flavored Kahlúa.

MAKES ABOUT 2 CUPS, FOR 8 SERVINGS.

10 ounces finest-quality semisweet (not unsweetened) or bitter-sweet chocolate, finely chopped
3 tablespoons unsalted butter
$1 1/4$ cups heavy (whipping) cream
$1 1/2$ teaspoons pure vanilla extract

In a heavy saucepan, combine the chocolate, butter, and cream. Place over low heat and cook, stirring frequently, until the chocolate melts and the mixture is smooth. Remove from the heat and stir in the vanilla. ➤

Serve warm, or cool to room temperature, then cover and refrigerate for up to 1 week. Slowly reheat, stirring frequently, over low heat or in a microwave oven.

Caramel Sauce

Simply sensational with warm chocolate cake or unfrosted apple or spice cakes. ❊ *Always devote your total attention to the process of caramelizing sugar. To prevent the melting sugar from crystallizing, do not stir it once it is dissolved until it is completely melted.*

M A K E S A B O U T 2 C U P S , F O R 8 S E R V I N G S .

2 cups sugar
1 cup heavy (whipping) cream
½ cup (1 stick) unsalted butter

Position a large bowl of iced water alongside the stove top.

In a heavy saucepan, preferably made of stainless steel or unlined copper, combine the sugar and ⅓ cup water and stir well. Place over medium heat, cover, and heat for about 4 minutes.

Remove the cover and continue to cook without disturbing the mixture until it begins to color, then continue cooking, slowly swirling the pan occasionally to spread the color evenly, until the mixture turns a rich amber; this will take about 8 minutes after removing the cover from the pan. During cooking, if sugar crystals begin to form around the sides of the pan just above the bubbling syrup, brush them away with a pastry brush moistened with water. As soon as the syrup reaches the desired color, briefly place the pan in the iced water to halt the cooking, then set aside.

In a heavy saucepan, place the cream over medium heat and bring almost to a boil. Stirring constantly, slowly add the hot cream to the syrup. Place over medium heat and stir constantly until the mixture is smooth. Remove from the heat, add the butter, and stir until the butter is melted.

Serve immediately, or cool to room temperature, then cover tightly and refrigerate for up to 2 weeks; slowly reheat, stirring frequently, over low heat or in a microwave oven.

V A R I A T I O N S

Caramel Syrup

Substitute 1 cup warm water for the cream. Omit the butter. Use for soaking cakes or as directed in recipes.

Chocolate Caramel Sauce

Finely chop 8 ounces bittersweet (not unsweetened) or semisweet chocolate, add it to the warm finished sauce, and stir until the chocolate is melted.

Coffee Caramel Sauce

Substitute 1 cup hot brewed espresso or other strong coffee for the cream, or stir 1 tablespoon instant espresso into the warm cream.

Nutty Caramel Sauce

Toast 1 cup pecans or other nuts as directed on page 123, then chop and stir into the finished sauce.

Thin Caramel Sauce

Prepare the sauce with water as in the Caramel Syrup variation, then add the butter.

Fresh Berry Sauce

Choose blackberries, blueberries, raspberries, strawberries, or other similar berries to make this simple sauce that complements plain cakes.

MAKES ABOUT 2 CUPS, FOR 8 SERVINGS.

4 cups seasonal berries

2 to 3 tablespoons sugar, or to taste

1 tablespoon freshly squeezed lemon juice or berry-flavored liqueur, or to taste

In a food processor, puree the berries. Pour through a fine-mesh strainer into a bowl to remove the seeds, if desired. Add the sugar and lemon juice or liqueur and mix well.

Serve immediately, or cover and refrigerate for up to 3 days.

Old-fashioned Dessert Sauce

My favorite way to enjoy gingerbread is how my mother always serves it: warm from the oven napped with this sauce. The simple preparation is also good with unfrosted chocolate and spice cakes.

MAKES ABOUT 2 CUPS, FOR 8 SERVINGS.

2 cups sugar

2 tablespoons cornstarch

2 cups milk (not fat free)

$\frac{1}{2}$ cup (1 stick) unsalted butter

2 teaspoons pure vanilla extract

In a small saucepan, combine the sugar and cornstarch and whisk to blend well. Slowly whisk in the milk. Place over medium-high heat and bring to a boil, stirring almost constantly. Continue cooking and stirring until the sauce is thickened to the consistency of cream. Remove from the heat, add the butter and vanilla, and stir until the butter melts.

Serve warm, or cover and refrigerate for up to 1 week. Slowly reheat, stirring frequently, over low heat or in a microwave oven.

Toasted Nuts

Toasting greatly enhances the rich flavor of nuts. Be sure that the nuts are fresh, and toast only as many as you need, as they turn rancid quickly.

Shelled whole or halved nuts or coarse pieces

Preheat an oven to 350° F.

Spread the nuts in a single layer in an ovenproof skillet or baking pan. Toast in the oven, stirring occasionally, until lightly browned and fragrant, 10 to 15 minutes. Except when toasting hazelnuts, transfer the nuts to a plate to cool.

If toasting hazelnuts (filberts), immediately pour the toasted nuts onto one-half of a cloth kitchen towel spread on a work surface. Fold the other half of the towel over the nuts and vigorously rub the warm nuts with the towel to remove as much of the loose skins as possible. (It is not necessary to remove all of the skins.)

Use as directed in recipes.

Grated or Shredded Fresh Coconut

Shake coconuts and choose one in which you can hear the juice inside.
MAKES ABOUT 4 CUPS.

1 mature coconut with juice inside

Preheat an oven to 400° F.

Using an ice pick or a nail, pierce holes in the three indented "eyes" on the top of the coconut, invert, and drain out the clear juice into a container. Taste the juice to be sure it is sweet; if rancid, discard and start with a fresh coconut. Reserve the good juice for another use (such as Soaking Syrup) or drink it as a cook's treat.

Place the coconut in the oven for 15 minutes, which usually cracks the shell and will cause the pulp to pull away from the shell for easier removal. Transfer to a countertop. If the shell did not crack from the heat, hold it with one of your hands and hit it with a hammer or the blunt edge of a heavy cleaver until it does. Using an oyster knife or similar instrument, pry the shell open. With the oyster knife or a dull table knife, pry out sections of the white pulp from the shell.

Using a small, sharp knife or a vegetable peeler, remove the brown skin from the white pulp, then rinse the pulp under cold running water to remove any brown fiber that has clung from the shell. Using a hand grater or food processor, shred or grate the coconut.

Use as directed in recipes, or cover and refrigerate for up to 2 days.

Fresh Coconut Milk

Unless you have access to high-quality frozen or canned coconut milk, prepare your own fresh version for making haupia *for the Hawaiian Coconut Cake (page 67).*
MAKES ABOUT 3 CUPS.

6 cups Grated or Shredded Fresh Coconut (left), unsweetened dried coconut (sold as "desiccated coconut" in natural-foods stores), or thawed frozen grated coconut
3 cups boiling water

In a bowl, combine the coconut and boiling water, stir to mix well, and let steep for 30 minutes. Working in batches, if necessary, transfer the coconut and liquid to a blender or food processor and blend until the mixture is as smooth as possible.

Line a strainer with several layers of dampened cheesecloth and set over a clean bowl. Pour the coconut mixture through the strainer, pressing against the coconut pulp with the back of a spoon, then wrap the cheesecloth around the pulp and squeeze to extract as much liquid as possible.

Use immediately, or cover tightly and refrigerate for up to 2 days. Stir to blend well before using.

Praline

Finely grind caramelized nuts, or praline, and mix into batters, fillings, and frostings to add a crunchy texture. Or coarsely grind or chop the caramelized nuts for pressing onto the sides of a frosted cake or sprinkling over the top as a garnish. ❄ *Always devote your total attention to the process of caramelizing sugar. To prevent the melting sugar from crystallizing, do not stir it once it is dissolved until it is completely melted.*

MAKES ABOUT 2 CUPS.

1 cup almonds, hazelnuts (filberts), pecans, or other nuts, or a mixture
Solid vegetable shortening, at room temperature, or cooking spray for greasing
1 cup sugar

Toast the nuts as directed on page 123.

Using a pastry brush, grease a baking sheet with shortening, or coat with spray, and set alongside the stove top.

In a heavy saucepan, preferably made of stainless steel or unlined copper, combine the sugar and $\frac{1}{4}$ cup water and stir well. Place over medium heat, cover, and heat for about 4 minutes.

Remove the cover and continue to cook without disturbing the mixture until it begins to color, then continue cooking, slowly swirling the pan occasionally to spread the color evenly, until the mixture turns a rich amber; this will take about 8 minutes after removing the cover from the pan. During cooking, if sugar crystals begin to form around the sides of the pan just above the bubbling syrup, brush them away with a pastry brush moistened with water.

As soon as the syrup reaches the desired color, remove the pan from the heat and stir in the nuts. Quickly pour the mixture onto the prepared baking sheet, spread the nuts into a single layer, and set aside to cool completely until hard.

Break the praline sheet into small pieces. Transfer to a food processor and grind to desired texture; do not overprocess or the praline will turn into a paste.

Melted Chocolate

Use the type of chocolate called for in recipes and always use low heat to prevent scorching.

Finest-quality bittersweet, semisweet, unsweetened, milk, or white chocolate containing cocoa butter, coarsely chopped

In a skillet or shallow saucepan, pour in water to a depth of 1 inch, place over medium heat, bring just to a simmer, and adjust the heat to maintain barely simmering water. Place the chocolate in a heatproof bowl, set the bowl in the simmering water, and stir the chocolate constantly just until melted and smooth; do not allow to burn.

Alternatively, place the chocolate in a microwave-safe measuring cup or bowl and microwave at 50 percent power for bittersweet, semisweet, or unsweetened chocolate or 30 percent power for milk or white chocolate, stirring every 15 seconds, just until melted and smooth; do not allow to burn.

Use as directed in recipes.

Recipe Index

INDEX TO CAKE RECIPES IN OTHER JAMES McNAIR COOKBOOKS

Table of Equivalents

The exact equivalents in the following tables have been rounded for convenience.

U.S.	METRIC	FAHRENHEIT	CELSIUS	GAS
$^1/_4$ teaspoon	1.25 milliliters	250	120	$^1/_2$
$^1/_2$ teaspoon	2.5 milliliters	275	140	1
1 teaspoon	5 milliliters	300	150	2
1 tablespoon (3 teaspoons)	15 milliliters	325	160	3
1 fluid ounce (2 tablespoons)	30 milliliters	350	180	4
$^1/_4$ cup	60 milliliters	375	190	5
$^1/_3$ cup	80 milliliters	400	200	6
$^1/_2$ cup	120 milliliters	425	220	7
1 cup	240 milliliters	450	230	8
1 pint (2 cups)	480 milliliters	475	240	9
1 quart (4 cups, 32 ounces)	960 milliliters	500	260	10
1 gallon (4 quarts)	3.84 liters			
1 ounce (by weight)	28 grams			
1 pound	454 grams			
2.2 pounds	1 kilogram			

U.S.	METRIC
$^1/_8$ inch	3 millimeters
$^1/_4$ inch	6 millimeters
$^1/_2$ inch	12 millimeters
1 inch	2.5 centimeters

Acknowledgments

To everyone at Chronicle Books for all their varied contributions to this book, especially to my longtime editor, Bill LeBlond, for reserving this subject for me until I found time to work on it, and to assistant editors Sarah Putman and Stephanie Rosenbaum for keeping everything flowing smoothly throughout the project.

To Sharon Silva for another vigilant and superb job of copyediting the text.

To Brenda Rae Eno for turning my words and pictures into a beautiful book.

To Carl Croft, Steve Fletcher, and Del Rimbey at Dandelion and to Iris Fuller at Fillamento for the loan of props from two of my favorite San Francisco stores. Thanks also to the courteous staffs of both stores for their help. To Frank Maxwell and Lois Hansen of Maxwell & Associates for the loan of KNF Designs and Vietri tableware, and to John Nyquist of Vanderbilt & Company in St. Helena, California, for arranging the loan.

To Brian Maynard at KitchenAid for the equipment used to make all of my cakes.

To my family and friends who shared recipes, loaned props, offered support, and evaluated cakes, including Almut and Rolf Busch; Scott Cameron; John Carr and Richard Ridgeway; Carla Carpentier; Mary Nell Coco; Ruth Dosher; Mark, Maile, and Malia Forbert; Carol Gallagher; Naila and Harold Gallagher; Larry Heller; Lynn Hickerson and Terry O'Flaherty; Christine High; Gail and Tad High; Ken and Kim High; Tanya High; Gloria Holden; Steven Holden; Laura Jerrard; Doris Keith; Connie Landry; Jane Lidz and Bill Johnson; Patrick Marks; Marian May and Louis Hicks; Lucille and J. O. McNair; Martha and Devereux McNair and John and Ryan Richardson; Peter Olsen; Jack Porter; Erika Rosenthal; Ann and Efren Santos-Cucalon; Kim, Jeff, Hailey, Max, and Cassidy Shapiro; Michele Sordi and Pamela Davis; Kristi, Bob, Alex, and Jody Spence; Blodwen Tartar and Alan May; Brooksley, Jim, and Cameron Wylie; Liana Weldon-Batten; and Mary Whitney. And to the casts of *La Verbena de la Paloma* at Jarvis Conservatory in Napa and *Of Mice and Men* at Opera San Jose for helping so many extra cakes disappear during testing and photography.

To Joshua J. Chew, Miss Vivien "Bunny" Fleigh, Miss Olivia de Puss Puss, Beauregard Ezekiel Valentine, and Michael T. Wigglebutt for their unwavering love and support.

To my partner, Andrew Moore, for his creative ideas, meticulous testing, careful editing, keen photographic assistance, and constant encouragement. *He takes the cake!*